The Pleasures of
DOG OWNERSHIP

The *Pleasures*

Also by Kurt Unkelbach

Love on a Leash
The Winning of Westminster
Murphy
The Love That Shook the World
Bink of Bullet Hollow
Ruffian: International Champion
The Dog Who Never Knew
The Dog in My Life
Both Ends of the Leash: Selecting and Training Your Dog
You're a Good Dog, Joe
Catnip: Selecting and Training Your Cat
A Cat and His Dogs

of Dog Ownership

By THE *Love on a Leash* FAMILY
Evie and Kurt Unkelbach

With a distinguished panel of canine authorities

Aennchen Antonelli § *Sam Gardner* § *Isabella Hoopes* §
Maurie Prager § *James Trullinger* § *Lloyd Case* § *Walter
Goodman* § *Elsworth Howell* § *Corinne Macdonald* §
Glenna Crafts § *Dan Gordon* § *Kae Reiley* § *Bill Watkins*
§ *Bernard Ziessow*

PRENTICE-HALL, INC., *Englewood Cliffs, New Jersey*

The Pleasures of Dog Ownership by Evie and Kurt Unkelbach
© 1971 by Evie and Kurt Unkelbach
ISBN 0-13-684597-5
Library of Congress Catalog Card Number: 72-145960
Printed in the United States of America *T*
Prentice-Hall International, Inc., London
Prentice-Hall of Australia, Pty. Ltd., Sydney
Prentice-Hall of Canada, Ltd., Toronto
Prentice-Hall of India Private Ltd., New Delhi
Prentice-Hall of Japan, Inc., Tokyo
Design by Janet Anderson

Second printing. . . . . August, 1971

TO
Tawn, Red,
Duke, Duchess,
Peanut, and all the
others we loved and miss

PREFACE

OUR *combined experience with dogs runs to something less than a hundred years. However, thanks to persons named and unnamed, this book reflects better than thirty-five hundred years of experience.*

All of the training and handling methods discussed herein have been tested and proved and may be considered within the limits of canine intelligence. Rest assured that the obedient dog does not learn through osmosis, and that a dog of any age can be trained. If he's to be a worthwhile pet and a pleasure to own, he needs a little training. He needs more training if he's to be a show dog. And he needs a great deal more if he's headed for the Obedience trials.

Today, more than half the American canine population is purebred. Almost all of the purebreds are eligible for the breed ring or the Obedience trials or both. Training the purebred for either sport requires only the intelligence to read. Speaking the English language is not necessary.

New pleasures await the owners of purebreds in the dog game. We hope this book will remove the game's mystique and eliminate many of the hazards on the road to success.

Evie and Kurt
Walden Folly
Connecticut

ACKNOWLEDGMENTS

WE are grateful for the cooperation of the noted dog fanciers, from A (Antonelli) to Z (Ziessow), whose wit and wisdom have graced the pages of this book.

Many other names known to fame in the dog fancy contributed to our cause. Space, libel, and ethics do not permit a complete listing, but we would be remiss if we did not offer our sincere thanks to Jack Baird, Henry Bernacki, Gladys Carr, Dr. Raymond Church, John W. Cross, Jr., Richard d'Ambrisi, Herm David, Alfred M. Dick, Joe Gallant, Robert Garrido, Ken Golden, Rosamond Hart, Dorothy Howe, Arthur Frederick Jones, Claire Leishman, Janet Mack, Evelyn Monte, Tim Murphy, Jan du Pont, John Prentiss, Bonnie Proctor, Joan Read, John Rendel, Lyle Ring, Alva Rosenberg, Wentzle Ruml, Jr., Leo Sullivan, William Trainor, Bert Tormey, Dean White, Don Wilson, Dr. Armour Wood, and Arnold Woolf. Also, our thanks to the American Kennel Club, Association of Obedience Clubs & Judges, Dog Fanciers Club, New England Obedience News, and Professional Handlers Association.

May the Lord bless all those who love dogs, and may He enlighten those breed judges who do not honor our own dogs, as we forgive them for their strange interpretations of the Labrador Retriever standard.

Evie and Kurt

CONTENTS

The Pleasures of
DOG OWNERSHIP

CHAPTER I

SOME DOGS THINK
THEY OWN PEOPLE

The sport of dogs, or the dog fancy § *The fine distinction between dog lover and dog fancier* § *Dominance of the female dog fancier* § *History of shows and the American kennel club* § *Qualifications for owners and canines* § *The importance of winning* § *speaking of England and other pithy remarks*

WELCOME to the dog game. May the best dog win, and we hope he belongs to you.

The game is known by many other names. Purists call it an amateur's sport, cynics insist that it's politics, laymen think of it as a beauty contest, and losers refer to it as one blind man's arbitrary opinion. And then there are those who depend on it for a living. They are sure it's a business.

But under any name, the dog game means the dog fancy. The fancy is international, and any American owner of a properly registered, purebred dog (of a breed recognized by the American Kennel Club) may claim instant membership. The owner's race, creed, color, age, political party, social and marital status, profession, creditors, intelligence, and criminal record are all unimportant. Truly a democratic society, although personal wealth can be a help.

Thus, anyone can become a dog fancier, and some five million living Americans claim that distinction. Not all are active in any given year, but once a dog fancier, always a dog fancier, and their active ranks are growing by leaps and bounds. For every face that disappears, two are waiting in the wings, and ten would be if more owners of purebreds were to investigate where the action is. It's at the dog shows, where proud owners prove that "my dog is better than yours," or that "my dog is smarter than yours," or both. Better in the sense that the dog is a superior physical example of his breed, and smarter in the sense that he proves his superior intelligence in a set of predetermined exercises. The breed ring tests his conformation, and the Obedience trial proves his brain-power.

Close to eleven hundred of these shows dot the U. S. A. landscape every year (plus another two hundred in Canada), and they are held indoors and out, in every season. All but eight are single-day events, and it's a seldom weekend when one or more shows aren't within easy driving distance of every dog owner. More shows are added to the schedule each year, and thus far only the Twelve Days of Christmas remain immune. It is as if all dog fanciers and their dogs need a rest at the end of the year. For some fanciers, of course, it is a welcome opportunity to become reacquainted with their children.

It is assumed that all dog fanciers are dog lovers, and some find it difficult to distinguish between the fanciers and the lovers. In our experience, the normal dog lover mentions his dog upon request, or tells some anecdote about his dog in the casual manner that he would discuss the weather. His love is a sort of private matter. The dog fancier doesn't wait for a question. He explodes with information about his dog's deeds, his own expert knowledge of the canine world, and subtle remarks about your ignorance. His love is in public domain. With cotton in one's ears, anyone should be able to distinguish a dog fancier from a normal dog lover at fifty paces. A fast (but hazardous) way to make the distinction is to insult a man's dog. The dog lover may or may not debate. The dog fancier will redden and punch.

"I can tell from her noise just how long she's been a dog fancier," an old-timer often told us. He was correct in both pronoun and theory. The female sex does dominate the dog game, and novice dog fanciers always seem louder than the veterans.

There's no real reason why the ladies should outnumber the men, unless there's more truth than myth to the old saw about women controlling the purse strings of America. In the beginning, or more than a century ago, men laid the foundation for the dog fancy. Most were men of wealth, for our earliest purebreds had to be imported from abroad. Sporting and Hound breeds were the popular imports at first, and their wealthy owners became the first serious dog breeders on this side of the Atlantic. They were the originators of our first dog shows, although they regarded the shows as friendly gatherings for the educational purpose of comparing one breeder's results with dogs of other breeders. The judge was always a breeder himself, and if he found more virtue in his own dogs than those of others, the competition understood that human nature is a fickle thing. Today, when a judge (who remains a breeder) gives a win to a dog that he sold as a pup a year ago, verbal rumblings are heard from coast to coast. It's a wise judge who retires as a breeder, especially if he's sensitive by nature.

In the light of history, those early shows were no more nor less than informal social events. It was pleasant to own a winning dog, but the breeders and their ladies were true sportsmen and weren't miffed when losing. Indeed, winning or losing was unimportant. The intent was to learn by comparison, and then to apply the new knowledge to the improvement of one's breed.

In spirit anyway, that original intent still exists today. This will come as a shock to hundreds of thousands of dog fanciers, but one of the official aims of the American Kennel Club is "The holding of dog shows at which purebred dogs may be exhibited and be given an opportunity to compete for prizes and thus enable their breeders and owners to demonstrate the progress made in breeding for type and quality."

Since many dog fanciers are husband-and-wife teams—indeed, they may have met at a dog show—it is not surprising that the first three words spoken by their babies are "American Kennel Club." This is, of course, the governing body of the American dog fancy. Without it, a chaotic state of affairs would exist, and the dog fancy would be in even more confusion than the cat fancy, which stumbles along with eight governing bodies.

The A.K.C. was founded in 1884, or just in the nick of time. By then, there were more pure breeds around, the dog fancy had slipped from the hands of the wealthy into public domain, shows were becoming popular events in the big cities and added attractions at country affairs. The shows were conducted according to the whims of their sponsors, the judges were often more familiar with cattle than dogs, and serious breeders were justifiably alarmed. By creating and enforcing uniform rules for dog shows, by setting a standard of perfection for each of the recognized breeds, by establishing the title of champion, by registering purebred dogs, and by scores of other measures, the A.K.C. brought order out of confusion and the dog fancy was on its way. Without it, we wouldn't have better than twenty million purebreds in this country today. Our total canine pet population would be far larger than the current forty million and constitute one hell of a nuisance. Owners of mongrels are not noted for controlled-breeding programs.

Since its inception, all of the officers of the A.K.C. have been men. The voting members are the delegates from the hundreds of member kennel clubs, single-breed clubs and Obedience clubs. All the delegates are male. Dog fanciers consider the club to be the last stand of masculine authority, but that is an illusion. Many of the delegates are really stand-ins for their wives, and receive voting orders from home. The day will never come, but if all the female dog fanciers went into retirement, the club would find itself vastly overextended.

Except for the fact that it is nonprofit, the club is more trade union than club, for its membership consists of other clubs. It takes about five years and quite a bit of persuasion to convince the average dog fancier that he is not a member of the A.K.C., but such is the case. In a sense, the fancier's dog is closer to membership than he is.

If litter registrations are in order (a responsibility of the breeder), then the purebred pup can be registered with the A.K.C. and shown in the breed ring at the age of six months. On that very day, the dog owner, for better or worse, is allowed to stop thinking of himself as just another dog lover. The very moment he steps into the ring with his dog he has both the legal and moral right to consider himself a dog fancier.

Well, the above is not quite that simple. A dog cannot be shown if he is vicious, blind, deaf, lame (even temporarily on show day), castrated, spayed, or changed in appearance by artificial means except as specified in the breed standard; further, a male dog must have two normal testicles normally located in the scrotum. In show parlance, the dog must be whole.

Thus, a dog is whole if he has all his parts in working order and doesn't try to chew up other dogs. The only variations are specified by the individual breed standards. A whole white German Shepherd Dog cannot be shown because he's white. A whole Collie sports the ears and tail he was born with, or as nature intended. A whole Boxer carries clipped ears and a docked tail, or as man decided to improve on nature. The several breeds forced to undergo tampering by man do not seem to mind and may be grateful. Take the Boxer again. With his natural floppy ears and natural long tail he looks more like a hound than a working dog.

Incongruous as it may seem, then, several breeds must have their ears cropped if they are to conform with breed standards. Only when they are missing portions of their ears are they considered whole. And if that sounds confusing, consider the fact that the cropping of canine ears is against the law in several states. The operation is performed at a tender age and the pup must endure a few weeks of pain. It does constitute cruelty to animals. Still, in the very states where cropping is against the law, breeders, owners, and veterinarians carry on with the practice. That's not the only blot on the dog fancy's escutcheon, but it's the biggest. The docking of tails can't be classified as cruelty. A kick on his rump gives a young pup as much pain.

So the show dog must be six months old, healthy, whole (in

accordance with his breed's standard) and a member of a breed recognized by the American Kennel Club. Of more than two hundred pure breeds of dogs in the world, the A.K.C. recognizes only 116. The magic number changes about once in a decade, as one breed is dropped or another is added. In this respect, the club moves with the speed of a sleepy turtle, making absolutely sure that an old breed is practically extinct before dropping it, and that another breed has gained enough popularity to stay around before adding it. Right now lobbyists for ten new breeds (old elsewhere, but comparatively new to this country) are clamoring for recognition:* Akitas, Australian Cattle Dogs, Australian Kelpies, Border Collies, Cavalier King Charles Spaniels, Ibizan Hounds, Miniature Bull Terriers, Soft-Coated Wheaten Terriers, Spinoni Italiani, and Tibetan Terriers. These breeds are seen today at many shows,† where they compete against each other for ribbons and constitute a sort of sideshow. The winning dogs cannot earn points toward championships, however, and making one's dog a champion is the real name of the dog-show game. Still, the new breeds are getting public exposure, one or two will probably be added to the recognized list by 1980, and by then addicts of another ten new breeds will be clamoring for attention. Most fanciers believe that we have too many recognized breeds right now, but there are always minority groups around lobbying for recognition of a new breed and hoping to make a fortune when people clamor for pups of the breed. To date, there's never been a clamor.

Chances are that the American dog fancy will not rest until there's a purebred dog in every home and the Queen admits that the British dog fancy is playing second fiddle. At our current output of about four million purebred pups a year, the first goal may not be an impossible dream. But replacing England as the number-one canine power in the world is something else again. While we do have more dog fanciers and more purebred

---

* The A.K.C., sort of acknowledging these breeds, lists them as Miscellaneous.

† To qualify, the dog must have an Indefinite Listing Privilege number from the A.K.C.

GENERAL VIEW OF THE BENCH SHOW IN THE HIPPODROME, ON THURSDAY, MAY 10TH.

D. P. FOSTER'S "LION"

JONES'S SIB. BLOODHOUND "BRUNO" 1' PRIZE

"DAGMAR" "OSCAR"
QUEEN VICTORIA'S DEER-HOUNDS, VALUED AT $100,000.

MR. JONES'S SIBERIAN BLOODHOUND "BRUNO."

McDONNA'S "ROVER" $50,000.00

'MUNGO'
THE REV. MR. MACDONNA, WITH HIS DOG "MUNGO."

WAGNER'S "NELLIE"

MISS B. WEBB'S "REX" $1000.00

O. MATHEWS'S "DUKE" $1000.00

JOHN MATTHEWS'S "DUKE," VALUED AT $1,000.

MR. JOHN K. T. GRAINGER'S SETTER "NELLY" AND HER PUPS, VALUED AT $5,000.

TWO-LEGGED DOG.—PUG "REX."—THE ONLY ESQUIMAUX IN THE SHOW

ESQUIMAUX DOG

The above sketch of the first Westminster Kennel Club Show appeared
in *Leslies Weekly*, in the year 1877. *American Kennel Club*

dogs and the world's oldest continuous dog show (Westminster Kennel Club, 1877), England boasts more recognized breeds, many more dog shows—including the world's biggest (Cruft's) —and more fanciers in high places. England exports more dogs, too, and commands higher prices. And what really hurts is this sad truth: most of those exported dogs are bought by American dog fanciers.

The majority of the dogs imported from England do not make their new owners happy. But when the price is right, or high enough, the British fanciers will part with their good ones, and every year a number of them lick the daylights out of American-bred dogs. Those few are the ones who are remembered, and they don't help American fanciers who are trying to overcome an inferiority complex.

Unfortunately, the tables cannot be reversed. For a long time the British had a handy defense against invasion by top American-bred dogs: a six-month quarantine law for all imported animals. No dog lover, seller or buyer, wanted to see his dog in prison for six months. The British law was not established as an act of discrimination against American dogs, although there are those who feel it was. It went on the books to protect the livestock of the British Isles against hoof-and-mouth disease, and was successful until recent years.* The only American dog fancier to thwart the quarantine successfully was, apparently, Xavier Cugat. He once told us that for years he smuggled his beloved Chihuahuas in and out of England by stuffing them into his overcoat pockets.

Time changes all things, of course, and today it is possible to find a few English canine authorities who confess that America is now superior in some of the breeds. Not all, but some, and the Terrier breeds in particular, "Of course," they always remind us, "you Americans did get your original breeding stock from England." That is a fact for most of our breeds, but a

---

* As of 1970, a new law placed Britain off limits to all foreign animals. Now everyone wants the quarantine to come back.

A typical morning scene during the breed judging at any Westminster. With ringside seats at a premium, gentlemen do not offer their places to ladies. A seated person who asks "What breed is this?" becomes an object of scorn. *William P. Gilbert*

majority of American authorities will agree that we now surpass England in most of them.

The minority, or those who find a certain status in owning British-bred dogs, disagree. For them, anything native will never suffice, be it dogs, fashions, autos, or wines. Most of the minority carry this to an excess, and don't even read the American canine journals. The best of ours are monthlies, but the best of the British are weeklies. That gives England one-upmanship in the literary field. The British also publish more dog books. Two-upmanship.

But whether he belongs to the majority or the minority, it's easy to distinguish a dog fancier from a normal dog lover if he has traveled to England. When he returns home, a conversation with a dog fancier will run along these lines:

"So you're just home from three weeks in England? Did you see any new plays in London?"

"I visited forty-five kennels."

The Working Group being judged at the Chicago International dog show, this country's biggest two-day event—the one most likely to overtake England's Cruft's and become the world's largest canine affair. The scene is 1968, the weekend following the Martin Luther King assassination, and riots were raging a few blocks away. Hundreds of entered dogs were absent. Thousands of spectators stayed away (note empty seats). The dog fancy is still debating whether this 1968 show should have been cancelled, as were so many other sporting events around the country.   *William P. Gilbert*

"What museums did you visit?"

"Lady Agnes Millstone told me that, judging from my snapshots, my Papillons were just as outstanding as hers."

"Did you buy any tweeds?"

"I bought three puppies."

"What did you think of the countryside?"

"I attended seven dog shows."

So like it or lump it, the American fancier remains in awe of his British cousin, and this feeling is not likely to change. The British are just as devoted, just as fanatic, and just as eager to own winning dogs, but somehow they have been able to retain the original spirit of the dog game: amateurism. The professional handler (one who will handle your dog for a fee) is an American invention. Today, he is not unknown in England and other countries, but only in America is he common rather than

A partial view of one of the biggest outdoor shows in the West, the annual Santa Barbara Kennel Club event. This one-day show draws over 3,000 dogs. *Eldon Tatsch*

the exception, and only in this country can he earn a prosperous living.

The British fancier handles his own dogs in the ring. He would do so from a wheelchair if the rules permitted. As it is, invalid fanciers find other amateurs to handle for them. As it was in the beginning, when only true amateurs handled dogs at dog shows, so it is today—in England.

And by comparison anyway, we must concede that British judges are amateurs. This does not mean that they are not qualified. It does mean that they cannot demand the high fees commanded in this country, and thus a judging assignment represents more of an honor than a payday.

So right down the line, England retains the amateur spirit. While in this country, the original intent of dog shows (improvement of the breeds) has been obscured, over there amateurism reigns supreme.

Here, every fancier is considered to be an amateur, but some don't work at it. It is almost axiomatic that the wealthier the fancier, the greater his desire to own (and not necessarily breed) winning dogs, and to place those dogs in the care of professional handlers. It's great to own winners, and to see one's name in the papers, and thus qualify as a noted sportsman.

Success in the dog fancy can be purchased, and it doesn't require brains. It is a simple matter of buying a great dog (and not just a good one), and agents are available for this purpose. Then the buyer shops around for the right professional handler, who is often the agent. From that point on, expenses run about five hundred a month and up.

This is the sure road to success in the dog fancy, if success is measured in terms of wins. One does not even have to know, ever see, or feed one's dogs. So it is a convenient way to gain fame, and also far less expensive than owning racehorses.

Fortunately for the average American dog fancier, it is not the only road to success. The great majority of our fanciers do their own handling, and often place their dogs over those handled by the top professionals. If the legion of active amateurs were to disappear, so would the dog shows and the dog fancy. It's the little fellow, the one- or two-dog owner, who supports the dog game.

The biggest one-day show in the East is sponsored by the Trenton (N. J.) Kennel Club. Seers predict this show will go over 4,000 dogs any year now, making it about two-thirds the size of two-day, indoor Cruft's. *Pure-Bred Dogs*

He finds pleasure in it. And so would tens of thousands of other dog owners if they only knew that their pets were fine examples of their breeds.

But sometimes it's difficult to convince a man that his Rover is a worthy beast. Tell him that his pet has the makings of a champion, and his reply will be along the lines of, "You must be kidding. He was the runt of his litter, and my brother gave him to us, and my brother never gives away anything of value."

It's best to talk to his wife. Tell her the same thing about Rover, and almost always she'll reply, "When's the next dog show?"

Women seem to have more intuition, and a stronger sense of pride. Maybe that's why they dominate the dog fancy. Or perhaps they have a stronger craving for pleasure.

They would seem to have more courage, too. Students of new faces at dog shows agree that the head of the house seldom accompanies Mrs. Jones and Rover to their first few shows. The husband remains at home, delighted to have free time for gardening, golfing, or drinking, and quite unaware that his care-free days are about to end. He joins his wife and Rover at about the fourth show, and from then on he's hooked. If Rover wins, he can't wait for the dog to win again. If Rover loses, he can't wait to put the dog under an "honest" judge. The fancy has two words for what happens: "dog fever."

The fever appears to be a saving grace for many marriages. Of all our special-interest groups, the dog fancy claims the lowest divorce rate. A friendly psychiatrist, a dog fancier himself, offers this explanation: "Once they become dog fanciers, husband and wife tend to find less fault in each other. Increasingly, they concentrate on other fanciers, other fancier's dogs, and judges. In my estimation, the fancy has saved countless thousands of marriages."

He was speaking from personal observation and experience. If he were on your couch, he would confess that his wife's Miniature Schnauzers were the difference between his happy marriage and divorce.

CHAPTER II

THE PEOPLE
PUREBREDS TOLERATE

Then and Now § Decline of the Big Kennels § Importance of Breeders and Amateurs § Professional Handlers and Their Role § Breed Judges, How They Fare, and Certain Observations and Anecdotes § An Explanation of Championship Points, Classes, Inconsistencies, and Personal Emotions § How Wealth Does Not Deter Success, and Other Thoughts

ON THE occasion of his fiftieth birthday, when he was already famous, and wealthy and aware of all the good things in life, the late Albert Payson Terhune wrote: "There is a thrill in competing for a dog show blue ribbon that is beyond the thrill of the best horse race."

What was good enough for Terhune is not good enough for the average dog fancier. The famous author of dog books experienced his thrills while standing at ringside and watching his Collies compete under the handling of professionals. He never knew the bigger thrill of handling one's own dog to a blue, or the greater thrill of handling one's own homebred to a purple ribbon, which is the name of the game, or championship points.

In his day, of course, handling one's own dogs was not the fashion. It was the time of big kennels and all the necessary trimmings: a kennel manager (preferably a Scot), kennel maids (preferably English), and a professional handler or two—necessarily American. The kennels were luxuries, of course, and none could possibly break even. Ownership was akin to social success, or a further embellishment of same.

That period is gone forever, but it shouldn't be forgotten. The big kennels flooded the dog shows with entries and kept the dog game rolling along. Through showing, they exposed and popularized many of the pure breeds. And they did import fine breeding stock from abroad, or the best that money could buy, and thus introduced worthy bloodlines that are behind many of the fine dogs known to fame today.

These days, the big kennels do not set the pace for the dog fancy. Cost is the controlling factor, and we have become a nation of small kennels, with actual sizes dependent upon the amount of free family time and labor available. The showcase operations that remain are in the hands of the very wealthy, but the wealthy represent a fraction of the dog fancy.

The above may not seem consistent with what one actually sees with one's own eyes. True, but kennels do abound and there will be more of them next year, and 95 percent of them have no interest in the improvement of the breeds and their owners should not be classified as dog fanciers. They are kennels in name only, puppy factories in a very real sense, and doing the fancy more harm than good. Prolific rather than serious breeding is their main objective, and they are in business to supply puppies to pet stores, department stores, mail-order houses, and laboratories. They supply purebred merchandise purchased by innocent dog lovers who believe that A.K.C. papers guarantee quality. They don't.

The thousands of fancier-breeder kennels run from two to ten adult dogs and produce from one to five litters a year. Brood bitches are not bred every time they come in heat, there are always a few retired veterans around, and breeding is never wholesale. If all owners of these small, more-or-less hobby kennels were forced to be honest about all things, few would claim a profit. As a matter of pride, most owners admit to a profit, but said profit is seldom noted on their income-tax returns. Conversely, losses are often entered and seldom allowed.

From our own experience, there's pleasure and satisfaction, but not dollar profit, in the ownership of an average-sized breeding kennel. Income from pups and services has rarely equaled overhead, and never equaled it when a fair price was set for family time and labors. Overall, the happy boasts of those kennel owners who do not board dogs should be taken with several grains of salt.

Almost all of the profitable kennels are also in the business of boarding, but this has its drawbacks. There's no guarantee, for example, that off-the-street dogs are free of contagious diseases. And some person must be present at all times, if only to guard against theft. The raiding of kennels to supply dogs for the black market supported by research laboratories (some operating on federal grants) is now commonplace all over America. And a boarding kennel is a violation of local zoning in a growing number of communities.

The steady increase in the number of small kennels can be traced in part to the growing demands of the public for purebred pups. A more important influence, however, is the ever-growing army of dog fanciers. Sooner or later, the active fanciers can't resist the urge to breed dogs, and thus new kennels are born.

Happily, today's average kennel isn't big enough to flood the dog shows with entries, and the kennel owner competes on the same terms as the nonkennel owner. He's just another amateur fancier, but showing his own homebred dogs rather than purchased ones, and enjoying the ultimate thrill when his dogs win.

Overall then, the dog game is in the right hands. It belongs to the amateurs, with about a five-to-one ratio in favor of the so-called weaker sex. The game is played by men, women, and children, and their dogs. If it sometimes seems to them that the professionals do all of the winning, it only seems that way. The professional resents losing, for winning is his bread and butter. When he loses to an amateur, it seems to him that there should be a law prohibiting amateurs from handling. This is a rather shortsighted view. If it weren't for the amateurs, there would be no professionals, for there would be no dog shows.

It is the amateurs who form and keep alive the kennel clubs

and breed clubs that sponser the dog shows, and often lose money in the process. And it is the amateurs who enter all the dogs at a given show. The majority handle their own dogs, whereas the few retain the services of the professionals.

There are now about five hundred professional handlers in the United States, and the best of them net over fifty thousand dollars a year. It's a pretty good life for anyone who doesn't mind being away from home on most weekends, has a talent for keeping clients happy when their dogs lose, can laugh at the rumors a professional inspires, and prefers the company of dogs to people. Since many dog fanciers feel precisely that way and the loot can be considerable, one may wonder why there aren't tens of thousands of professionals.

The reason why is the American Kennel Club. One cannot handle for a fee without obtaining a handler's license, and obtaining that license is getting tougher all the time. It doesn't hurt to have a college degree, a fine family name, and a friend in the White House, but it doesn't help, either. What does help is the applicant's background as a breeder, his experience as a handler of a breed or breeds in the show ring, his character, his standing in his community, his record as a responsible human being, and his physical setup for maintaining dogs. If the applicant impresses on those counts and others, he is granted a limited license* that permits him to handle certain breeds. As time goes on, and if all goes well, he picks up more breeds, and the limits become less limited and eventually the limited license becomes a full handler's license. Then the professional has nothing to worry about except finding clients and keeping them happy. They aren't too hard to find. Keeping them happy is something else again.

All this does not mean that all professional handlers are angels, but since licenses are not easily come by these days, the overall quality has improved. Many fanciers resent them, feeling that the dog game should be for amateurs only. To them, it is as if a Baltimore Colt could play on a high-school football team.

But the professional is here to stay. For good or for evil, he

---

* About half the professionals hold limited licenses.

is a convenience for those who can afford his services, and is extremely valuable to those whose egos demand that their dogs win, if not all of the time, at least almost always.

Love them or hate them, the professionals are on hand at every show and the established ones are the only fanciers who earn big money in the dog game. Full-time, that is.

Part-time, many dog-show judges earn decent money in the dog game. Only the most ardent dog fanciers become judges, and they must qualify and be licensed by the A.K.C. to judge one, more, or all the breeds. The applicant's actual profession does not matter. Thus a breed judge can be a banker, lawyer, plumber, tree surgeon, farmer, schoolteacher, or washwoman. Once licensed, he or she becomes a free agent in the art of acquiring fees. In the beginning, the fee may amount to no more than travel expenses. Later, it can amount to hundreds of dollars a weekend.

The boom in dog shows has not been accompanied by a flood of new judges, and experienced judges of many breeds are so much in demand that they rake in five hundred dollars and up for their labors on a Saturday and Sunday. That's pretty fair avocational money, and often more than they earn all week at their vocations. Thirty or forty such weekends a year are not unusual for a popular judge, nor are bookings two and three years in advance. It takes from five to ten years for a judge to become popular, the criterion being the power of his name in attracting a large entry of dogs.

For the clubs sponsoring dog shows, the number of dogs entered in breed competition is all important. It spells the difference between loss, breaking even, and a small profit. The entry fees (eight dollars per dog is now average) is the show's chief source of income which must cover such major expenses as judges' fees, ground rental, show superintendent, catalogs, trophies, and promotion. This holds true for the growing number of limited shows, too—limited in the sense that only a certain number of dogs can be entered, the usual cause being limited space. Classic Westminster, for example, could probably draw ten thousand dogs for its annual event, but limits entries to three thousand. (To hold down an epidemic of entries, only champions and dogs with at least one championship point are eligible for Westminster.) But for the majority of the shows, indoors and outdoors, the more dogs the merrier, and popular judges attract them.

All breed judges play second fiddle to a group of about thirty who are known as all-rounders. They are licensed to judge all of the 116 breeds recognized by the American Kennel Club and are regarded as the elders of the dog game. It is a common complaint in the dog fancy that some of the elders eld for too long, or until they can no longer walk into the ring. Salaried officers of the American Kennel Club are edged into retirement at sixty-five, but judges remain active as long as they are physically able. Avocation knows no retirement age.

There was a time when only the all-rounder could judge Best in Show. Then, with new shows popping up all over the land, the demand for all-rounders outran the supply. Today a Group Judge (one licensed to judge all the breeds in a given Group) is permitted to handle Best in Show honors. This means that about one third (five hundred) of the active breed judges are eligible to give the final verdict at shows, and there's no longer a shortage.

But no matter how many breeds he's licensed to judge, the breed judge is limited to looking at no more than 175 dogs per show. This limitation has upped the overhead for the small shows, which must now provide more judges than before, and entry fees have jumped and will continue to jump. The moral, if any, may be that what's good for the judges is good for the fancy. And since there are many husband-and-wife teams in the dog game, the limit on their labors may make for happier lives at home. Judges are very critical of each other, but rested judges are less so. "Did you see what my wife put up in Pointers today? Scandalous!" one overworked judge used to tell us. But now he is not overworked, and he has changed his tune to "My wife knows more about this breed than anyone else in America, including myself."

Today, only licensed judges judge the breeds, but this was not true before 1970. Until then, professional handlers were permitted to judge at specialty shows. Thus, the sponsors of a Poodle specialty might engage the services of a professional famous for his handling of top Poodles. This was rational, since the professional probably knew more about the breed than the average Poodle judge. It was also sneaky, for the handler would have to leave his top Poodles at home and other dogs would win the honors. And maybe it wasn't cricket, for some poor judge had lost an assignment. Well, somebody up there, and the judges plead innocent, had the rule changed, and now professional handlers must stick to their own thing.

While judges outnumber professional handlers by more than a three-to-one ratio, every professional does not own three judges at a given show. Appearances are deceiving. The whole truth is that a top professional handles only top dogs, and he wins with them more often than not. He may think that the Boxer Rebellion was a dog fight, but he does know a top Boxer from a pretty good one, and he is careful to enter his dog under a judge who also knows Boxers from end to end. The judges he avoids are the ones who don't see the dog through his eyes.

If judges have it so good, if the pay is fine, the work short, and all expenses paid, then why don't most dog fanciers become judges? The qualifications are tougher than those demanded of a professional handler, the apprenticeship is more demanding, and a long, successful background as a breeder is essential. While a few veteran professionals switch to judging, almost all judges come from the ranks of active breeders.

At any given time, thousands of fanciers qualify for the role of judge, but fewer than one in ten thousand decide to take the plunge, and not every one of them makes the grade. Of all the people in the dog game, the judges are the most discussed—and cussed. The rules of the game are such that there must always be more losing dogs than winning ones, and human nature guarantees that there will always be more sorehead than gladhead owners.

It is the purpose and solemn duty of the breed judge to select the dog who comes closest to the breed standard* and to declare

---

* A written description of a perfect specimen of the breed.

that dog a winner. Unlike dog fanciers, all judges must be able to read and write, but a dozen judges may interpret the same breed standard differently, even as twelve witnesses of an accident testify differently in court. It takes a few years for the average dog fancier to understand this. When he does finally understand it, he hopes that the judge who does not interpret correctly (that is, the way *he* does) and give his dog a win will get lost. Oddly, about half of the dog fanciers are not familiar with their favorite breed's standard. "I don't know anything about art, but I know what I like" doesn't work when applied to the dog game.

At the end of each assignment, and depending upon the size of the show, the judge can, if he so desires, add a dozen or a hundred names of new critics to his life list. If he is a methodical man, he can place the names under column heads: fanciers, professionals, other judges, and spectators. So the judge, if he is to retain his sanity, cannot be a sensitive man. And that's as good a reason as any for the reluctance of many fanciers to seek judgeship. The fancier is rare who can stand criticism of his own dog. Criticism of himself? Never.

It is written in stone that the judges who stay in the game attract both an army of critics and popularity. As the years roll along, the dog fancy's grapevine spreads the line on every judge from coast to coast, and popularity is achieved. Kennel clubs vie for his services at their shows, and fanciers rush to enter their dogs under him for the very reason he attained his popularity: he does know and stick to the breed standard, and thus every dog under him will get a fair break; or he is erratic, and one never knows if he will be consistent or not, and thus any dog, including the worst one present, stands a good chance; or he is not a "handler's judge" and thus will give a dog handled by an amateur a good look.

As the judge moves along in his dog-game career, the experts in each breed start analyzing his popularity in terms of specifics: in Labradors, for example, he prefers black over yellow, or vice versa, but never chocolate; he likes giant or small size, or doesn't gave a damn; he does or doesn't know proper movement; he'll always go for an English import over an American-bred dog; or

his concept of short-coupled is found in the Dachshund.* Good
or bad, the specifics cannot be proved in court, but they belong
to the judge for the rest of his days.

Thus, a judge's popularity, general or specific, becomes his
reputation in the dog game and does not necessarily mean that he
is admired or loved. But no matter his reputation, his may be the
most profitable avocation known to man. It is also safer than gam-
bling and a fine way to see the country without expense, sometimes with one's mate.

The thinking dog fancier pays little or no heed to the grapevine
and makes up his own mind about the judges, basing his decision
on experience and observation. Up ahead, we'll note our own
method of rating Labrador judges. While not ours alone, it has
worked for us and saved a great deal of time, travel, and money.
It is mentioned here because it led to an interesting discovery
about a minority of judges in many breeds who interpret not
only the standard in their own wild fashion but also the rules of
the game.

Bear in mind that many judges remain as breeders. Then ponder
the first Golden Rule of the A.K.C. It specifies that persons cannot
be judges who "Buy, sell, and in any way trade or traffic in dogs
as a means of livelihood, in whole or in part." If one works for a
kennel or sells dog food or owns a pet shop, then he cannot become a judge. How can the judge who continues to breed and
sell pups and dogs not be trading and trafficking in dogs?

The A.K.C. takes the long view: " 'Trade and traffic in dogs'
does not refer to the normal activities of a breeder who sells
surplus dogs of his own breeding or re-sells dogs bought for
breeding purposes." So far, so good. The key word, it would seem,
is "normal."

The personal interpretation of the word has given some judges
plenty of latitude. It is almost as if they sought the status of being
a judge to expand their breeding activities. If they did not seek,
they soon discovered that the title "judge" could be employed as

---

* See Chapter XII, *Parlance.*

a sales tool, and they went to town. In truth, they are earning their livelihood from dogs.

When does a breeder-judge overstep the bounds of normalcy or propriety? It's a sticky question, and everybody, including the overstepping judge, has a different answer. For our money, we feel ethics are involved when the judge uses both hard sell and implication in the quest for the almighty buck. One of the current lady judges, and never mind her breed, is in the habit of advising new fanciers that she has sure-winning pups for sale and of assuring new breeders that her stud dog is the only right stud for their unlikely bitches. Personally, we'll never forget the day a judge invaded the sanctity of our home in an effort to sell a pup to a guest of ours. We wouldn't have minded, but the guest had driven a thousand miles to buy a pup from us.

If the word "implication," as mentioned above, puzzles anyone, it does not puzzle the A.K.C. One of its hard-and-fast rules is that a dog owned and sold by a breeder-judge cannot be shown under that judge for twelve months. This is no hardship for anyone buying a pup from a judge, of course. It takes a year for the average pup to develop his potential anyway.

Happily, the very existence of the A.K.C. rule indicates an awareness that hanky-panky does exist. Dog fanciers by the tens of thousands hope that the rule will be changed, in their lifetimes, from twelve months to something like forty-eight months. There's hardly a fancier alive who would wait that long to show his dog under a particular judge.

In defense of the breeder-judges who have turned their avocation into a profitable business, it must be admitted that they are patriots of sorts, in that they hate to see the good American dollars drain in the direction of England. For too many years now British judges have condescended to arbitrate at U. S. A. dog shows in return for handsome fees (the reverse is not true), and usually they come well supplied with photographs of British canines. It's no trouble at all for the honored visitor to show these photographs to wealthy American dog fanciers, arrange sales, and return home wealthier by several handsome finder's fees. It is only necessary to add that many of the dogs thus procured and imported do not always live up to the promises of the departed judges.

Once upon a time, an American judge decided to teach the Britishers a lesson in their own backyard. He had an educated eye for top dogs, the Terrier breeds in particular, and twice a year he visited the important English dog shows and looked over the new crop of pups and young adults. He kept careful records of the dogs he liked. "I put them in pickle," he used to explain, "and look at them again six months later. Then, if I still like them, I make the necessary arrangements." The arrangements consisted of buying the dog for wealthy American dog fanciers, whom he also kept in pickle. The English sellers were delighted to cut the judge in on the swag, and the clients were happy to pay him a finder's fee. So the late pickler profited from both ends of the arrangement.

Meanwhile, or as time permitted, he accepted judging assignments on this side of the Atlantic, and quite often—and finally once too often—he found his winner in a dog that he had discovered in the British Isles. Somebody complained (the owner of a losing dog was suspected) and the A.K.C. removed the prospering judge's license.

"What happened?" we once asked him.

"I've been put in permanent pickle," he replied. He was not unhappy, and devoted the rest of his days to a full-time career as the world's only professional canine scout.

So those are the people of the dog game insofar as the breed ring is concerned: the amateur fanciers, the amateurs who hire professional handlers, the professional handlers, and the judges. All are important, and all are engaged in a sort of undeclared social warfare at the dog shows. In the fancy, these are known as point shows, or the only place one's dog can pick up points toward the title of champion. The amateurs vie with each other and the professionals, the professionals vie with each other and don't worry much about the amateurs, and everybody is out to win. And it's the judges, of course, who decide which dogs will win and which will lose. They are often at war with their consciences, for sometimes there isn't a whisker of difference between two top dogs, and only one can win. And always, always, there must be more losers than winners.

More losing dogs than winning dogs, that is, although—in the first flush of victory—the fancier considers himself the winner, and not his dog. When his dog loses, then the dog loses. The fancier never loses.

Point shows fall into two divisions: all-breed and specialty. At an all-breed point show, dogs of all 116 breeds may compete. A specialty show can be one of three divisions: (1) for a single breed, such as the Borzoi, and often held within the framework of an all-breed show; (2) for all the breeds under one flag, such as the nine breeds of Spaniel; (3) or for an entire Group, such as the seventeen breeds belonging to the Toy Group.

The point show—from start to finish—follows a simple process of elimination. In each breed ring, the judge declares a winner for the following classes:

Puppy: six to twelve months of age, whelped in the U. S. A. or Canada and not a champion. This is the starting class for most dogs.

Novice: six months and over, whelped in the U. S. A. or Canada, but ineligible after winning three times in this class, or after winning once in the following classes, or after winning one championship point.

Bred-by-Exhibitor: six months and over, whelped in the U. S. A. and not a champion; must be owned wholly or in part by breeder(s) or spouse of breeder(s) of record; must be handled by owner or member of owner's immediate family. Breeders often start their dogs in this class.

American-Bred: six months and over, whelped in the U. S. A. (by reason of U. S. A. mating), and not a champion. The starting class for many adult dogs.

Open: six months and over. Imported dogs must be shown in this class. Otherwise, the competition usually consists of dogs with championship points. Champions may be shown here, but that happens rarely.

Now all the blue-ribbon winners, or one for each class, meet to determine the best of the lot. The winner of winners receives a purple ribbon designating him as Winners Dog. Only he can win championship points; depending on the total number of dogs entered in all the classes, he can win from one to five points or no points at all.

Gentlemen are judged before ladies in the breed ring. Once Winners Dog is declared, the process of elimination in all five classes begins again, this time for the bitches. The best one present becomes Winners Bitch, and she, too, wins points in accordance with the total number of bitches in competition.

To win a championship, a dog or bitch must accrue a total of fifteen points. Since five is the maximum number of points to be won at one show, a championship title cannot be won at fewer than three shows, and a dog capable of even that accomplishment should be suspected of greatness. It happens, but not very often.

The fifteen-point truth is not the whole story, but many newcomers to the fancy believe that it is. The joys of owning a winner are such that some fanciers continue to show their dogs until total points of twenty or thirty have been amassed. They wait and wait for the A.K.C. to declare their dogs to be champions, and the day never comes. Only then, when they are on the verge of suing the club, do they take the time to learn that two of the dog's wins must be majors, and the majors must be won under different judges.

A major is a win of three, four, or five points. So at least six of a champion's points must be majors. The other required nine can be picked up as one- and two-point wins, and at least one of those wins must be under a third judge. Thus winning twenty points at twenty shows under many different judges does not make a champion, so long as the two major wins are lacking.

The point scale is variable. It is not the same for every breed. Generally, the more popular the breed, the more dogs required per point. Thus, in German Shepherds, seven class dogs must be present for Winners Dog to earn one point, and thirty-three must be in competition to make the win worth three points, or a major. In Pugs at the same show, two dogs compete for one point and only seven for a three. The scale of points for bitches may or may not be the same. All very simple, but often confusing to a dog fancier for two or three years. Especially when he learns that what's true in New Hampshire may not be true in Florida. The A.K.C. has divided the nation into four regions,* considered the breed totals of the regions, and made the necessary adjustments. And all point scales are revised on an annual basis. What was true last year for Rough Collies in Maine may not be true this year, although it may be the same for Idaho.

Back in the breed ring, where the judge found his Winners Dog and Winners Bitch, the process of elimination begins all over again. This time the object is the title Best of Breed. The two winners compete with champions of record for the title and purple-and-gold rosette, plus whatever trophies and cash go with the honor of being declared the day's supreme representative of the breed. More often than not, neither of the two nonchamps takes the breed.

But wait! Even in defeat, one of the two has another honor coming: a blue-and-white ribbon denoting Best of Winners. The win may or may not be important. If the dog has just won more points than the bitch, and now she is declared the Best of Winners, then she forgets her points and assumes his. The reverse is also true. It is a matter of equal rights.

In the end, one dog or bitch per breed is declared Best of Breed. At the Saw Mill Kennel Club (N.Y.), that is also the end of the dog show. At all the others, the excitement is still ahead. The Best of Breeds proceed to their respective Groups for further elimination.

There are six such Groups: Sporting, Working, Hound, Terrier, Toy, and Non-Sporting. The elimination begins again within each Group and continues until a winner for each is declared.

These six finalists enter the day's final elimination. These, in the opinion of the judges, are the six best dogs in the show. It is always a minority opinion, of course. Deep in his heart, the owner of the worst Beagle in the show feels that his dog should be in there. All the owners of the other eliminated dogs feel the same

---

* Plus separate point schedules for Alaska, Hawaii, and Puerto Rico.

way. Most of them smile, however. It is part of dog-fancy tradition to win modestly and lose graciously, or smilingly, and sometimes overdoing it a bit by grinning from ear to ear.

The judge points to the winner. That dog is Best in Show. That
winning dog or bitch stands supreme and can win no higher
honor, unless it be another Best in Show at an even bigger show.

A strong man weeps when his dog wins Best in Show. A woman
throws away her hats. She has no need for them. Now she wears
a halo, although only she can see it. To own a Best in Show dog
is the dream of every dog fancier who ever lived. Sadly, most die
without realizing the dream, but that sober fact doesn't diminish
anyone's yearning.

In theory, any man, woman, or child can own a BIS dog. The
dog-show world is truly democratic. In actuality, the wealthy
fanciers who prefer canines to racehorses and yachts have a distinct advantage. At present rates, five to thirty thousand dollars
will buy a great dog. Always, a top professional handler is available—at a price. After that, all it takes is a young fortune to campaign the dog (or dogs) from coast to coast. It is not a guaranteed
way to obtain dogdom's Holy Grail(s), for money cannot buy
a judge's decision—but no better way has been devised to date.

Why, then, doesn't the dog-show world fall flat on its face or
become the exclusive game of the wealthy? Because the records
show that fanciers of average income and less also handle their
dogs to BIS. In the past decade, about 30 percent of the BIS dogs
were handled by owners who found themselves short of cash
each April 15.

It seems strange to the layman that a single canine expert, the
judge, can select one of six dogs as the very best and worthy of
BIS. After all, each of the six has already been declared best of
his breed and best of his Group. Why, then, are all not equal?
What is this, a beauty contest? How can a perfect Great Dane
be better than a perfect, tiny Maltese? Is the Great Dane superior
because there's more of him, and thus more of perfection?

The layman's confusion isn't helped when the next day, at another show and under another judge, the very same Maltese takes
BIS over the very same Great Dane. That's why the general

public views dog shows as beauty contests, and only dog fanciers disagree. They are familiar with the magic three words that explain all: ON THAT DAY.

On that day, meaning the first show, the Great Dane showed the judge something that the other five dogs didn't. On that other day, or the second show, the Maltese did the extra showing.

It is usually difficult to nail down the judge on just what did influence his BIS decision. It is not the case in England, but in this country judges are wary of making detailed explanations. At best, on that day, a judge wins at most two true friends: the owner-handler of the BIS dog, or the owner and the professional handler. The judge does not want to offend the owners of the other five finalists. Still, the press, the public, and the fancy want him to say something, however brief.

One of our little hobbies has been the collection of BIS judges' quotes, as reported in the press and the canine journals. Among our favorites:

"I had a difficult time deciding, but the Basset Hound did have a touch more of spirit." This is regarded as a safe, rational statement, for all fanciers know that dogs are similar to people, in that one cannot be in extreme high spirits every minute of every day.

"Each of the six finalists deserved the BIS. I selected the Pekingese bitch because I've bred Pekingese for thirty-five years and never seen a better one." An honest judge, but she didn't help her own popularity any.

"I was not influenced by the fact that the Irish Setter drew the most applause. A coincidence. I would say that the Setter's superiority was obvious to all." Better left unsaid.

"The difference was in coat. The Collie's was in beautiful bloom. By the way, I just learned that he's a grandson of my own Champion Golden Glow, who went BIS ten times." Better to have given BIS to the Skye Terrier, whose coat was even longer and bloomier, and whose grandfather was unknown to the judge.

"Six great dogs, but the Saluki gaited like a dream." We were present on that day, and the lady judge was sporting. As she examined the bite of the Saluki, he nipped her.

"I was not aware that the Welsh Terrier was a class bitch. She was my obvious choice. The others had too many faults." An honest and unique statement, and probably the reason why it was another two years before the judge received his next BIS assignment.

His BIS winner was unusual, but not rare. Most of the BIS dogs are champions, but sometimes—or often enough to cause hope to beat in the heart of every new dog fancier—a dog does come up from the breed classes and go all the way to Best in Show. When that happens, many dog fanciers at the show become aware, for the first time, that points can also be won at higher levels than the breed.

The nonchampion Welsh bitch who went BIS makes a handy clarification. On that day, she had won Winners Bitch in the breed ring. The win was worth a single point. Winners Dog was worth three.

She went on to take Best of Breed, giving her an automatic Best of Winners. Now, having defeated Winners Dog, she was credited with three points.

As Best of Breed, she went on to the Terrier Group and won. With the win, she was entitled to the highest point rating of any breed in her group on that day. In Airedales on that day, Best of Winners was worth four points. Now the Welsh forgot her three points and accepted four.

On to Best in Show. In taking BIS, she was entitled to the highest point rating of any breed entered in the show that day. A young army of German Shepherd Dog bitches had competed in breed for five points. Although a German Shepherd was not among the six finalists, the Welsh Terrier went home with five points. A nice win, and an unusually big one for a class Welsh Terrier. In popularity, the breed usually ranks around fiftieth, and finding enough competitors to win a major at any given show can be a problem.

It was not that particular bitch's first breed win, but it was her first major and first and only BIS. She finished her championship a couple of months later and won several more Best of Breed ribbons and placed, but didn't win in group competition.

It all happened seven years ago. Her owner is a personal friend, a dog-fancy member in good standing for more than a quarter century, and a Welsh Terrier breeder for most of that time. She's still a dog fancier and still eager for that next BIS. "But it won't break my heart if it doesn't come," she insists. "In a way, once should be enough for any dog fancier. It does something for you. All my life, I hated rainy days, but I don't mind them anymore. I cuddle Sarah and we remember the time we won Best in Show, and the sun seems to shine. Really, a BIS is life's greatest gift, and I think more dog fanciers should have it, and that the American Kennel Club should limit one BIS per person. Such a wonderful feeling! You know?"

We don't. Not yet anyway. What we're looking for is a judge who knows Labradors inside and out. An honest judge who bred Labradors for about forty years, but who retired as a breeder some years ago. Somebody like that BIS-Pekingese judge we quoted.

CHAPTER III

A TITLE
IN THE FAMILY

Recognizing a potential champion § *The Breed standards* § *Kennel Blindness* § *Testing at Match shows* § *where to Go for Expert Advice* § *Judging patterns at point shows* § *Junior showmanship* § *Buying a pup* § *Educated Guesses* § *Jitters* § *Advantages of proper Line Breeding* § *common complaint of Handlers*

WHILE the changeover from dog lover to dog fancier is an instant sort of thing, knowledge does not necessarily accompany the act. Most novice dog fanciers plunge into the action with little experience in the art of handling and an overblown estimation of their dog's quality. It all looks so simple, but enthusiasm and love are not enough.

Once in a thousand times, a novice and her Lhasa Apso will win a point or two at their very first show. "I don't know how I did it!" she will proclaim, not realizing that the other dogs in competition did not resemble an Apso—for one Apso looks like another Apso to her—or that the judge was in a hurry to catch a train. She may never win again, but the thrill will keep her in the dog game for a long, long time, and chances are that her handling will remain atrocious forevermore.

So most of the novices lose for a few shows or many, and a few retire. The latter blame their dogs or dishonest judges, but never themselves. But until the day they die, they will consider themselves breed experts.

"If he can't stand losing, then he doesn't belong in the game" is the sound advice of Tom Gately, the veteran professional handler. Tom (now retired) has been offering it without charge for over thirty years. Nobody has argued with his logic, but hardly anyone has followed it. The more a fancier loses, the surer he is that winning days are just around the corner. The professionals, of course, are always walking on thin ice: any dogs they handle must win with some frequency, or the clients become unhappy. And winning the breed won't keep some clients happy. They want to win big, or at least take Group every time out and maybe BIS. When a client's dog takes one or both at a show, he is happy to hand over the preagreed bonus to the happy pro.

Winning is a pleasant way of life, but it's a wise dog fancier who takes losing days in stride. There will always be more of them.

Fortunately, the dog fancy has a built-in method for assuring a minimum of losing days up ahead. It's called the match show.

In the dog game, the Big Time—the Palace of days gone by—is the point show. The match show is small time, or the proving ground, or the Lyceum in Sweet Bend, Idaho.

There are three times as many match shows as point shows. All but a few are sponsored by the same clubs that stage the point shows. Most are sanctioned by the A.K.C. and abide by that body's rules and regulations.

A dog cannot win points at a match show. Ribbons are won and sometimes trophies, but never points. Otherwise, both match and point shows run along the same lines.

There are other differences but none of great importance. Match shows are small affairs and conducted in a more informal manner. Breeders and veteran fanciers are usually the judges. While licensed judges do not consider match shows beneath their dignity, they do prefer paying assignments. All services rendered at a match show are gratis. Usually, when a licensed judge donates his time and talent, a little investigation will reveal that he sells insurance and an officer of the sponsoring club has just purchased a policy. And sometimes, if the pressure from local clients is strong enough, a professional handler will serve as one of the judges.

Since match shows are held when there's no date conflict with nearby point shows, fanciers attend them to brush up on their own handling and to introduce their new hopes to the dog-show world. About a third of the fanciers at any match show know their way around and a third of them can be counted on to dispense logical advice to newcomers.

Then there's always a large group whose members may be the world's most rabid dog fanciers. In this cult, one finds the faces one used to see at the point shows. Unable to win, and knowing no more now than they did five years ago, these fanciers and their dogs have retreated to the match-show world. There, since the competition is not as stiff, a fair, veteran show dog should be able to defeat a green dog of quality who is handled in awkward fashion.

In a sense, they represent the dog fancy's second echelon. They are happy and eager to talk and advise, and should be avoided by anyone with serious intentions of advancing in the dog game. How to recognize a member of this cult? Well, he may rush right up to you, give his unsolicited opinion of your dog, forget to introduce himself, but introduce you to his scrapbook. The ribbons pasted in that book will be colored rose or orange or pink-and-green or lavender. And the lady who declared, "One of my dogs went Best in Show at Green Valley last Sunday!" should be suspected. Ask her, "Was that a match show or a point show?" She should have announced, "One of my dogs went Best of Match." There's a big difference.

The second-echelon cult can and should be avoided. Otherwise, the match show is the perfect start for the newcomer to the dog fancy. From the judge, he'll receive a fair appraisal of his pure-bred's quality. After three or four match shows, the fancier will have garnered the opinions of several judges and met a few breeders and veterans who will, upon request, offer their observations. Winning with one's purebred is pleasant but meaningless at this stage of the game. The judges mean well, but their decisions are informal and should cause neither a victory celebration nor alarm. What's important is getting a fair idea of your purebred's good points and faults, and becoming familiar with the meaning of such terms as "hock," "bite," "topline," "angulation," "stifle," and "cow hock." Meanwhile, one learns a bit about ring procedure and handling by simple observation.

A pup is eligible for most match shows at the age of six months.* The one danger is his exposure to so many other dogs, for a few of them, thanks to witless owners, may carry disease. So the pup, or the adult dog, should be up-to-date on his immunity shots. The other end of the time spectrum for a starting adult dog is five years.

To avoid embarrassment and delay in the breed ring, any dog headed for his first match show should be trained to lead and collar, and capable of gaiting and standing firm. As we shall see, it doesn't take much intelligence to train any dog properly in those maneuvers. A week or so of short sessions usually suffice.

After a few match shows, the fancier will have more than a dim idea of his dog's chances in the Big Time. He will have a much better idea if he studies his breed's standard, understands it, and then compares his dog against it. A Standard of Perfection exists for every one of the pure breeds recognized by the A.K.C., and all may be found within the covers of the club's official publication, *The Complete Dog Book*. Most libraries carry it, all fanciers should own it (but don't), and it's easy to buy, borrow, or steal a copy.

It is the memory of a breed's standard—man's written description of the perfect dog of the breed—that the judge carries into the ring with him. His ultimate winner is, in his opinion, the dog who comes closer to the standard than all the other dogs in competition.

But it is never that simple for the owner. In his opinion his dog fits every word of the standard. The more he paid for the dog, the surer his conviction. This mixture of pride, love, and non-objectivity is known as kennel blindness. The dog's faults (if any) are minor and his virtues are major. It is difficult to overcome

---

* A few match shows permit younger ages.

kennel blindness, and sentimentalists never do. The dog game is full of them. They don't enjoy losing, but friends and neighbors know that they own show dogs and thus must be canine experts. It is a status sort of thing, and after all, if you don't play golf, why not spend your time at dog shows on weekends?

Blessed are the newcomers who are not entirely kennel blind. When they compare their pride and joy with his standard, they do find inconsistencies or faults. They realize that, just as there are no perfect mortals, there are no perfect dogs.

Now the question of the dog's chances to win his championship becomes more apparent. If he's an adult, and his faults are glaring and numerous (wrong bite, overlong tail, poor eyes, loose shoulders, swayback), his chances may be regarded as nil. If he's a puppy, then he may outgrow some of his physical faults. All one can do then is wait.

If doubt exists about proceeding to the point shows, then expert opinion should be sought. There are far more self-appointed dog experts in this country than dogs, and everyone can count two or three among his friends. Forget them, for friends tend to flattery. The other choices:

1.) *Your friendly veterinarian.* Usually a poor choice. While vets are experts on canine health and repair, few are breed specialists. When a vet says, "What a beautiful Lhasa Apso!" remember that the doctor called you a beautiful baby.

2.) *Owner of pet store.* One of the best sources of unqualified knowledge. The very few exceptions are themselves breeders of note and sell only their own pups.

3.) *Judge of the breed.* A fine choice, but don't be disappointed if he declines. Some are happy to oblige, for they feel they are helping the fancy. Others become indignant. They express their opinions only in the ring, if then. But if you find a cooperative judge and he likes your dog, don't feel your dog is sure to win under him. A superior dog might be present on the day.

4.) *A breed fancier.* A good bet if you happen to know one who has handled at least two dogs to their championships.

The land is full of one-champ owners who never learned anything about the breed. In most cases, the dog was too good to be denied, despite atrocious handling.

5.) *Your dog's breeder.* Well, this depends upon the breeder and his program. Science and the years have proved that proper line breeding produces the best results. This amounts to the breeding of related dogs through several generations, with all said dogs carrying desired dominant characteristics. In effect, the Mendelian theory. Thus strong points are bred in, and weak points erased. However, line breeding can also be improper, in that related bums are bred, and the result is more bums. A proper breeder, or the one who knows what he is doing, has usually produced his share of champions, for champs are one way of enhancing his reputation. Thus, he won't con you into showing your dog if he believes the dog doesn't stand a chance.

6.) *Any breeder.* Look for a veteran in your breed who has produced champions. If he doesn't like your dog and tries to sell you one of his pups, don't be heartbroken. Keep trying until you find a breeder who doesn't try to sell you a pup.

7.) *A professional handler.* Again, seek a veteran, and one who has had success handling your breed. Don't bother him at dog shows. Phone him, make an appointment, and expect to pay a fee.*

8.) *A complete stranger met at a dog show.* The ones who offer to evaluate your dog are the ones to avoid. Ninety-nine percent of them are experts in their opinion only. Caution! Don't drag Rover to a dog show in the hope of finding a judge or handler. Only dogs entered in the show are permitted on the show grounds.

Now, regardless of your own estimation and the opinion of the experts, you are ready for the Big Time. Not your purebred, but you. Attend a couple of point shows and watch the judging of

---

* A member of the Professional Handlers Association is the best bet. Don't take his opinion seriously if he expresses a desire to handle the dog for you. Sometimes flattery and business go hand in hand.

your breed. Observe the handlers, and note that at no time do they block the judge's view of their dogs. Observe the judging routine: first all the dogs are gaited, then they stand in line for his personal inspection, and next each is gaited individually. Then the crucial moments come: the judge takes his last looks, rates the best four dogs present, and places them one through four. Number one, of course, is the class winner. The judging pattern is traditional, and varies little from judge to judge.

We recommend this groundwork because you might as well know what's expected of you before getting your feet wet. If you've read this far and you own a purebred, you're probably going to show him at least a few times, regardless of expert opinion. And why not? The experts have been wrong before, and they will be again. In the final analysis, the judge in the ring is the only authority. Even in the case of unanimous negative opinions, there's still fun in showing a few times, and no harm in hoping that the experts were wrong.

The hope should not be eternal. If your dog hasn't won a blue ribbon in competition, or come close after four or five shows, it's time to stop dreaming of making him a champion. But for heaven's sake, don't despair. There's still a place for him in the dog game. One is Obedience (see Chapter VIII). Another, in the event you have an offspring or two, is Junior Showmanship.

Junior Showmanship is one reason why the dog game keeps growing. It amounts to a development program for the new blood, or boys and girls (ages ten through sixteen) who will mature into a new adult crop of dog fanciers. The new generation competes in various age brackets in a setup similar to that of the breed ring, but there comparison ends. Twenty youngsters, each handling a different breed, may be in the ring at the same time. The judge selects human rather than canine winners. His objective is to find the best handler in the ring.

Novice classes exist for beginners, and they stay in Novice until a first place is won. From then on, the Novice winner competes in Open, where the competition is more experienced. A total of five Open wins in a given year qualifies a juvenile handler for the JS finals, held annually as a feature of the Westminster

Kennel Club Show in Manhattan. These days, about forty thousand young fanciers compete at the point shows, but only about fifty individuals qualify for the finals. About two thirds of the finalists wangle time off from school (in February) and compete, and one (usually a girl) emerges as the winner and new Junior Showmanship champion of the world. It is too early to judge the end results of the attendant fame, but thus far none of the winners has become a movie star, written books, or tried to take over the A.K.C. Indeed, all those we know have remained normal individuals and continued as dog fanciers. In some cases, however, their parents are still up in the clouds and have become conversational bores.

Almost all point shows feature JS competition, as do most match shows. The latter, of course, are fine training grounds for beginners, although the wins are meaningless for qualifying. In the Big Time, the dog handled by the child must be owned by him or a member of his family. Thus, if you are doubtful about your dog's chances in the breed, the dog can still be a help to Junior in JS.

Most dog fanciers who are parents approve of JS, since it gives their children something to do at the dog shows. They are aware, too, that England's dog shows do not have JS. It is an American institution, and a fine way for American children to practice one-upmanship. We happen to entertain mixed feelings about the true worth of JS. So much depends on the personality of the individual child. He is going to lose more often than he wins, and if he can't take losing, he's better off at home.

In our own case, we found a handy use for JS by employing it as an award for good conduct, school grades, and the accomplishment of assigned chores. In addition, children are more conscientious than adults in the training of dogs, especially when they have an objective. So we had spare time for other endeavors, and think rather kindly of JS. For all we know, it may also have been the chief reason for keeping our growing daughters away from bad company, television, and LSD. So JS can have fringe benefits for family life.

It can also provide surprises. Two of our Labs, which we did not consider breed-ring candidates, went to the shows for JS chores. Since they had to be entered for the breed ring anyway, the girls were permitted to handle them there, too. Before long, both dogs had won their championships. Fine examples of the fact that a handler is all important to a dog's success. The real secret of the professional handler's success is his talent for showing off a dog's good points while hiding his faults. And that's why fair or good dogs can win over top dogs, although not every day in the week.

Sooner or later, the true dog fancier wants a champion canine in the family. Somehow, JS and Obedience accomplishments aren't enough. The yearning for a champ is mild in some cases, an obsession in others, and usually it ends in a frantic, quick search for a pup "guaranteed to win when ready." Thousands of those pups are always available. The trouble is, they seldom achieve the state of ready.

Most pups are sold between six and ten weeks of age. The seller who guarantees a future champion at those ages is not the most reliable man in town. At best, the guarantee is no more than an educated guess.

Each pup in a given litter matures at his own pace and in his own way. Thus a pup who looks like a sure winner at ten weeks may develop into a lost cause, whereas his sister, a hopeless-appearing bitch, may blossom into a sure winner.

The educated guess is best made by the line breeder who knows the dominant physical characteristics he's looking for and can spot them at the proper time. He must know what to look for and when to look for it, and those talents aren't easily come by. Time proves him right or wrong, and after several generations of pups, he becomes attuned to his strain and learns to guess right most of the time.

Overall, every line breeder hopes for one or a few sure winners in each litter. The dream, of course, is to produce a litter of champions. That can be done and it sometimes is done, but for the average breeder it depends too much on luck and promotion. It means selling only to people who will show their pups, egging them on to do so, and then praying that the poorer pups will find themselves in poorer competition often enough.

With our Walden strain of line bred Labradors, we make our guesses at five weeks and the long run has proved us right about 80 percent of the time. We have learned to look for breadth of head, heavyset tail, boxlike body, bone, spirit, and a few other secret ingredients. The ones meeting those qualifications are set aside for fanciers, breeders, or ourselves. The rest are available for owners interested in dogs for field, Obedience, or pet. When we learn that one of those has developed into a show champion, it's always pleasant news, and further establishes the fact that even the educated guess isn't always right.

The next best thing to the educated guess may be Madge Ziessow's program: "Instruct your brood bitch to have only one offspring. See to it that the pup gets fat from too much mother's milk, or so fat that he can't stand on his feet and moves like a turtle. Next, he must become ill and live only because of his fat reserve. Then try to sell him and fail. Finally, give him away to a kind relative."

That's the early story of a Lab pup named Dark Star of Franklin. Despite the fact that a previous breeding of his sire and dam had produced several outstanding offspring, nobody wanted to buy this only child. So Madge gave the sad-looking pup to her father. A couple of months later, the pup's parts grew into place.

While still a pup, he became Ch. Dark Star of Franklin. From there, in a brief eighteen months, he went on to one hundred Best of Breeds, eighty-five Group placings, forty Group firsts, and eight Best in Shows. His BIS wins were a record (1955) for the breed, and for many years no other Lab came close. Finally, the record was broken by a famous English import.

The important point is that both dogs were products of line breeding. In the long run, it's the line breeder who offers the best source for a winning dog. Through trial and error, every one of them develops his own formula for picking the right prospects.

Why, then, aren't all breeders practitioners of line breeding? It is one of the mysteries of the dog game, proving only that there is great diversity among fanciers. It is as if some people think Kentucky Derby winners are found in hack stables, or a prize bull is an accident of nature. One simply cannot convince otherwise rational people that breeding is a science.

One of our old acquaintances has been breeding Boxers in willy-nilly fashion for some fifteen years, and is famous for her lack of success. "I don't care what anybody says," she tells us about every six months. "I love every Boxer ever born. A Boxer is a Boxer to me, and the hell with the breed standard. I refuse to read it. And after all, I always sell my puppies." She does sell, no denying that. The pet stores adore her.

"Astrology dictates my matings, and there's no better way," a banker's wife told us. Except for coat color, her Golden Retrievers now resemble Otter Hounds. We withdrew our account from her husband's bank, rushed home and studied our records. One of our finest litters was whelped in 1963. The dam was a Leo and the sire a Scorpio. Via phone, we transmitted this information to the lady, saying that we were about to breed the two. She called back the next day and advised against it.

"Breeding is all a matter of luck," according to an old-timer in Airedales. "Luck and the law of averages. If I produce enough pups, I'm bound to have a few winners." We estimate that this kennel has produced about nine hundred pups. Five became champions. A line breeder would call that a foolish law of averages.

As the night follows the day, the wise fancier will find his right pup at the kennel of a proper breeder. The buyer should state his aim in honest fashion: "I intend to show my pup and make him a champion." The words will both please and stun the breeder. Please him, because here's somebody else who will show a dog of his strain, and stun him because nine out of ten times he hears, "I just want a pup as a pet for the kids."

The pet-pup approach is based on the mistaken theory that the asking price will be lower. This is in conflict with the breeder's point of view. In terms of dollars, one pup costs him just as much to bring into the world as another. And each pup is on equal terms with his litter mates so far as health, intelligence, and temperament go. As pets, none of the pups will run around town biting people and inviting lawsuits. For show or pet, a quality pup is never a bargain. How he is used is up to the new owner.

Usually, a litter of correctly bred pups carries one price tag for either sex. Some breeders will bring the price *down* on a top pup if the buyer pledges to show him. When the pup matures and is shown, he represents a free advertisement for the kennel. A male pup may go for a lesser price in return for future stud privileges, or a bitch pup might be available on a coownership basis. Breeders are always looking to the future and can't always afford to retain as much breeding stock as they desire.

Indeed, some of our best kennels are hardly kennels in the physical sense. The breeder may have only one or two top brood bitches, plus a single outdoor puppy run. Conversely, a big kennel with four or five litters running around should be considered a risk. It's a wholesale operation and depends upon that old law of averages.

Any kennel tells its own story. If stalls or runs are dirty, if there's the smell of dog in the air, if shy pups are cowering in a corner (they may be sick), if the breeder looks like somebody you wouldn't introduce to your own mother, then promise to return on another day and fail to keep your promise.

Except for the rare breeds, proper kennels can be found in every sector of the land. If you can't find one through normal channels, the nearest kennel club will help.

Whether you now own the right purebred or intend to own one sometime in your future, he's eligible for the point shows at six months of age. If he has a few match shows under his belt and you've done additional homework with him, then both of you will get along in the Big Time.

Just don't expect to set the world afire at your very first show. It's best to regard that one and the next few as orientation week in the dog fancy's school of higher education.

Winning points the first time out is always the exception. Your dog will find the show a new world and be more interested in the noise and activities than your commands. And you, despite your higher intelligence, will be nervous and not at your best.

Actresses are nervous the first few times they handle in the breed ring. So are politicians, schoolteachers, salesmen, journalists, retail clerks, and others who are accustomed to dealing with the public. Nervousness may be the hallmark of the true dog fancier. Some never conquer it, although they manage to hide it somehow. So it's perfectly proper to be nervous.

The true cause of the jitters has never been defined. It can't be the presence of the judges, for they are ladies and gentlemen. It can't be the action, for losing is not a death sentence. It could be the spectators. They observe the proceedings in the ring as if they were watching the final act before the world ends.

When the exception—the nervous fancier winning with his dog the first time out—happens, frustration is usually born. Dot Murphy, now a leading breeder of German Shorthaired Pointers, started as an exception. In her confession, she admits to being a nervous wreck at her first show. She does not remember how she managed to get her dog into the ring in the nick of time, or how she managed to get through the judging ordeal. "I stumbled into the judge once and almost fell on my dog," she recalls. Still, her charge went Winners Dog for two points.

The whole game looked simple to her. She continued showing, but her dog didn't win again. With each loss, Dot's nervousness increased, and finally her husband figured she was on the verge of a breakdown. Should he shoot her, the dog, or that first judge? The solution was a professional handler. He finished the dog in four straight shows. With a champion in the family, life returned to normal. Today, Dot handles her homebreds, admits to nervousness, but has learned to disguise it.

It is widely believed that a handler's nervousness is transmitted down the lead to his dog. We may be the only dissenters in the fancy. We do not believe this. If it were true, almost every dog in the breed ring would be nervous, and that's just not the case.

What might be true is the thought that the dog game is directly responsible for the increased sales of sedatives.

CHAPTER IV

JOURNEY
TO GLORY

Interesting Aspects of the Point Show § *Timing, Preparation, and Feeding* § *Sportsmanship and Friendships* § *Little Black Book on Judges* § *The Professional spirit* § *Tales of Judges* § *British standards* § *The Grapevine* § *Notes on savagery, criticism, interpretations, and conflicts in the Dog Game*

Point shows are held indoors and out, depending on date and locale. We happen to prefer the outdoor shows. Parking is easier, fresh air is pleasanter, and nature seems to absorb some of the noise. No matter the acoustics of the building, an indoor show sounds like a good battle.

Both man and beast are responsible for the din. Of the hundred breeds of dogs likely to be present, a score are noted as barkers and are quiet only in the ring. At all other times, the dogs never shut up. In order to be heard by friends three feet away, their owners must shout. This encourages the dogs, and they increase the volume of their soundings.

An innocent spectator might think that the dogs are unhappy. Not at all. If anything, the dogs are simply proclaiming their spirit. The successful show dog must have spirit, and he can't show spirit unless he's happy.

A late President was responsible for the canard that show dogs are treated cruelly and thus lead unhappy lives. The baseless statement grew into a belief that persists today in uninformed circles— but it just isn't true. The canine's natural needs, habits, and instincts are closer to man's than those of any other animal, domestic or wild. A man can't beat spirit into his wife or into his dog. Attention, affection, and kindness produce the joy known as spirit in all dogs and almost all women. The trick, with dogs anyway, is to keep them spirited without spoiling them. This is done by treating them like children, and not like equals or superiors. If your children are spoiled, we wouldn't know what to suggest.

Aside from training the dog, the requirements for entering him at a given point show are simple. Every show has an announced closing date, and an entry form (per dog) plus fee must reach the show's superintendent by that date. Obtaining the form is also a simple matter (Chapter XI), and no one should have trouble filling it out. A week to ten days before the show, the dog's official certificate of entry and an assigned number arrive in the mail. The certificate is the dog's admission ticket to the show grounds. The assigned number appears on the armband worn by his handler in the ring. The armband is supplied at the show.

In theory, the dog's number is his badge of equal opportunity. The judge does not know any of the dogs in the ring, and marks his book by the numbers, rather than by the names of the various dogs. This, of course, exonerates the judge from charges of favoritism. In fact, and more often than not, the judge has seen many of the same dogs before and knows their owners. But numbers are a speedier way of handling the official results, and the theory keeps most fanciers happy.

Every show has its catalog. In this, every dog's number can be found opposite his owner's name, his own registered name and A.K.C. number, his date of birth, his breeders, and his sire and dam. Thus, there is no chance that the official record of a win by Otter Hound 9 will be credited to Otter Hound 15.

Whether a point show is held indoors or out, it is designated in advance as "benched" or "unbenched." At a benched show, all dogs are assigned stalls which they are expected to occupy during certain hours. They are excused for exercising or judging, but otherwise are on display for the edification of spectators who consider that day lost when they cannot stare at every dog entered in a show.

The great majority of the shows and most of the outdoor shows (except for the giants) are now unbenched. This is a fortunate trend, doesn't seem to hurt the gate, and makes the day less of an ordeal for fanciers and their dogs alike. It also makes a shorter day for most of the owners and their charges. Dogs are usually excused when no longer required for competition. All breed losers, then, may head for home, and that means most of the dogs at the show.

Still, benched shows will always be with us. "The true purpose of a dog show," says a misinformed authority on the West Coast, "is to educate the public on the true worth of the purebreds. Where else can one see so many breeds close up?"

"Close up" is one of the reasons why we seldom appear at the benched shows. At several, we came around the corner just in time to find kind strangers feeding our dogs such tidbits as sauerkraut, frankfurters splashed with mustard, assorted candies, and other food not designed to help the dog's performance or health. At one show, we found our dog in cramped quarters. Some loving parent had parked twin babies with him.

A special, inexpensive piece of equipment is needed for benching a dog. This is a bench chain—long enough so that he can move about, but short enough to keep him from hopping off the bench. We prefer a folding bench crate, easy to carry and set up. Human nature is such that the average stranger doesn't quite trust a dog in a crate and passes him by.

For dog fanciers, the folding crate is one of man's finest inventions. At home, it can serve to confine a sick dog, or be used as his permanent bed. For travel, it's an ideal place to keep him, and the big reason why dog fanciers prefer station wagons. At the shows, benched or unbenched, it's a familiar place for him to rest. Crates are available in sizes for every breed.

If not planned, the first point show can develop into an exasperating misadventure. Experience is the best teacher, but here are the basics for a pleasant outing:

Timing. Predetermine the precise road route to the show, estimate the travel time, then add a half hour—just in case. By the time you are within a mile of the show's site, signs will start appearing and point the rest of the way. Plan to arrive at least one hour before your breed is ready to be judged. That should leave sufficient time for parking, unloading, finding the right stall at bench shows or a proper crate site at an unbenched one. Lacking a crate, search for a comfortable place. At outdoor shows, dogs may be kept in cars until needed or brought into the tent provided for handlers. Keeping the dog out of sunshine and resting him is important.

The mailing that brings the dog's entry certificate and breed number will include a judging schedule that informs you as to the proper ring for your breed and the time of the judging.

Once at the show, keep abreast of what's happening in the proper ring. If classes are small, the judging will move along in rapid fashion and your breed will be in the ring right on schedule. Absentee dogs are just out of luck.

About a half hour before ring time, it's wise to take the dog to the designated exercise area and hope that he'll answer nature's call. There's no law against his answering nature's call while he's in the ring, but it isn't considered proper and is bound to delay the judging.

Feeding. Both mortals and dogs must be considered. Mortals first: pack sufficient food for yourself. One of the hallmarks of a good dog show is that the food is terrible and high priced. This makes all shows good shows. Coffee, milk, and soft drinks are always available. If the inner soul demands hard liquor, pack that, too. Bar service is a seldom thing at dog shows. As for the dogs, we hold to the old tradition of feeding on schedule the day before a show, and not again until after the show. This almost guarantees no accidents in the ring, and an empty stomach keep a dog on his toes and alert for baiting, a ring procedure described on a future page.

Denying him food for a few hours won't hurt a healthy dog. Indeed, many professional handlers attending two shows on successive days with the same dog do not feed at all on the day of the second show. They claim a day of abstinence each week is splendid for any animal, although they do not practice it themselves. The manufacturers of prepared dog foods disagree.

Water is another matter. It serves as oil for the dog's body functions and a healthy canine will stay in the pink of condition for days on water alone. While fresh water is available at all shows, many fanciers bring along their own supply. As with humans, some dogs are affected by strange water—not on the day of the show, but on the following days. Diarrhea can be one of the end results. On long trips, we carry a native supply and a pan, and pause en route to give the dogs a small drink and a bit of exercise. On short trips, just the pan goes along, and we buy milk at the show. Milk seems to be a better thirst quencher, especially on hot days, and it does have a touch of nourishment. A panting dog in the ring is never at his best. Our Welsh Terrier friend carries mineral water for her dogs, ginger ale for her chauffeur, and rum for herself. Of late, she has been adding a few drops of rum to the dogs' water. "It keeps their muscles warm," she explains, "and they move beautifully in the ring." To each (fancier) his own (drinking system).

Packing. With the exception of the dogs, we stow all necessary gear for the show in the car the night before departure. This gives us plenty of time to ponder over what we have forgotten (collars, leads, scotch, pans, curries, tobacco, rabbit's foot) and minimizes confusion at takeoff time. If we remember to add the dogs, we're in good shape.

Many a fancier packs this private resolution: "If my dog doesn't win at this goddamn show, I've had it! I'll never take him to another one." He means it, but not deep in his heart. It is not easy to free oneself from dog fever. The dog game is rich in disappointments, but richer in fascination.

For that reason, even bitter fanciers carry a secret paper in their purses or billfolds. On it is the technical information concerning their dogs that will be needed when filling out an entry form for a future show. Somewhere on the show site the show's superintendent will have set up headquarters. There, premium lists and entry forms for future area shows may be found. Entries can be made on the spot. The fancier saves the price of a stamp, and a few pennies saved here and there are no laughing matter these days. Once a fancier's name has appeared in a few catalogs, he'll find himself on the mailing list for future shows. After that, the nonthrifty can make out entries in the comfort of their homes.

The alert newcomer to the fancy soon realizes that the dog game is not all sweetness and sunshine, and that the road ahead can be bumpy. The game, if not taken too seriously, can be stimulating, educational, and rewarding. It can mean the beginning of lasting friendships, a means of achieving normalcy (every normal person is supposed to have a hobby), and a broadening of one's knowledge. Unfortunately, about 70 percent of the players take the game very seriously. It seems to dominate their lives.

Overall, the big trouble with the dog game is not the dogs. It's the people, and a little understanding of them is better than no understanding at all.

Despite overlapping, three distinct classes of people constitute the dog-fancy society. They have been mentioned before: the amateur fanciers, the professional handlers, and the judges. Most of the amateurs do their own handling, the professionals handle for those who do not, and some of the judges handle when they're not judging.

Time, experience, and observation are the ingredients for the following, philosophical conclusions:

Fanciers. One of the great traditions of the dog game is sportsmanship. This is best illustrated in the breed ring, and just after a class has been judged. The losing handlers say, "Nice win," to the winning handler, or convey the same meaning with a handshake or a smile. And then there are losers who convey their congratulations to the winner by stalking from the ring, swearing, or mumbling something about the winner being a third cousin of the judge's wife. It is obvious that there must be degrees of sportsmanship.

The dog fancy welcomes all newcomers with open arms. At your first few shows, you will note that the warmest reception comes from fanciers in your own breed. They will be enthusiastic about your dog, helpful in all ways, and deeply interested in your latest operation. Soon a few will become your dearest friends, and you will be exchanging dinner invitations and learning more than you ever knew about your breed. As true sportsmen, they will confide the names of judges whom they sincerely believe will love your dog.

Beware! The more your dog loses, the more popular you become. The more dogs in competition, the more the points. The test of your new friendships will come on the day when your dog licks their dogs, and he takes home the points. Chances are that your dear friends will become just plain friends or acquaintances. Oh, you'll see them at the shows and talk with them, but some of the warmth will be missing. You and your dog now constitute serious competition.

In the long run, your lasting deep friendships will almost surely develop among fanciers of other and perhaps similar breeds. English Setter fanciers do appear to be cozy with the Irish's devotees, and there's a certain close bond between the Cocker Spaniel and English Cocker Spaniel clans. Alaskan Malamute and Siberian Husky fanciers are apparently born for each other. Only the Poodle people are inconsistent: the Toy owners don't seem to develop friendships in the Standard set, and fanciers of the Miniatures walk alone.

Ten to one, your true friends will be found in other breeds. If you're lucky, they will not consider the dog game a matter of life and death. "I really don't care if my dog wins or loses," a very popular phrase in the dog game, usually identifies the speaker as an intense life-and-deather. He considers the saying a sign of sportsmanship.

Professionals. Since it is a business, rather than a dog game, to the professional handler, it is not quite fair to consider him in the light of sportsmanship. Still, the P.H.A. code of ethics does call for "sportsmanlike conduct" at all times, so perhaps it is fair.

Well, some do and some don't display obedience to that particular effort. If morals really meant anything anymore, then one would think that the most prosperous handlers would be the sporting ones, but such is not the case. What with running a kennel, seeking new clients, pacifying old clients, and being away at the shows so often, a few of the big earners can hardly find time to dash to the bank. There just isn't time to read the code.

Few of the professionals are frank about their philosophies of life, but now and then they are revealing. Not so long ago, a leading lady among the professionals addressed a meeting of the Dog Fanciers Club in Manhattan. Since the club's roster is composed of the East's leading fanciers, it was her big chance to win friends and influence new clients. "Don't talk to us about sportsmanship! Listen, this is bread and butter to us. I go into the ring with one purpose in mind: TO WIN! I do everything within my power to win, and I feel like hell when my dog loses."

Her honesty shocked the audience of purists. All had been around long enough to know that's the way it was and is, but none wanted to hear it or believe it. The lady, by the way, is truly a lady, but not inside the ring. A lovely woman, even if she has bumped into our dogs on several important occasions.

Many handlers, of course, do not devote full time to the trade. They hold steady jobs and derive supplemental income from the game. Over the years, one such gentleman has worked for a single client: a fancier who doesn't mind winning, but who doesn't contemplate suicide whenever her dog loses. We assume that the arrangement has been pleasant and profitable, for the handler, a mannerly person of exceptional talent, has consistently turned down tempting offers from other hopeful clients. For years, we considered him the exception to the general rule, or the one professional lacking the must-win-at-all-costs attitude—a perfect gentleman inside and outside the ring. Then he confessed, "I love everybody, but inside the ring I would outtrick my own mother. My dog must win every time!" His tricks are many, and he has few equals in masking glaring faults in a dog. A devoted student of his breed and a patient trainer, he has made champions out of some pretty bum dogs. During the minutes he spends in the ring with a dog, he does (visually) improve the breed. So it is with all the top handlers.

With ten to thirty dogs of different breeds in his string, a good professional is one of the busiest individuals at a dog show. Last-minute grooming, instructing assistants, and rushing from one ring to another to handle different dogs doesn't leave him much time for lengthy conversations with friendly fanciers. Thus he is often regarded as a rude, uncooperative, heartless s.o.b., but that description does not fit the vast majority.

Fanciers determined to finish (make champions of) their dogs, but who are too nervous or too inept to handle successfully, often turn to a professional in the hope that he can accomplish the task. This works out more often than not. While this can run into real money, there is an economy method acceptable to some of the best handlers. It's called ringside delivery: at the proper time and breed ring, the owner hands over his dog (trained, groomed, and otherwise ready) to the handler. For a set fee (ranging upward from twenty dollars), the handler takes the dog into the ring. To the owner (if the dog wins), go the ribbons and trophies. Cash prizes are retained by the handler. If the dog goes on to Best of Breed, some handlers expect a bonus. If the dog goes on to win his Group (unlikely for a class dog), all handlers expect a bonus. And another bonus is due if the dog attains the impossible, or Best in Show. Owner and handler settle the bonus matter before the action begins. Neither believe it will come into play, and the odds against it are monumental, but the slim chance exists that a few dollars can run into a few hundred.

Long experience and success with the breed are a professional's best qualification with your dog, but that's something like a casting director advising freshmen actors to gain Broadway experience before trying out for a Broadway play. So the right handler may not have been around too long. Overall, the ones to avoid are those who approach you at a show and say, "You have a fine dog, but you'll never finish him, and I can." Those are the hungry ones. Before making a commitment, test the professional's sincerity with a shot of truth serum.

Judges. It is the duty of the judge to select the dog closest to said dog's breed standard. Ideally, the winning dog comes closest to perfection in that he has a minimum of faults. In practice, the judge may pick the best bum present, and that's why strange-looking beasts can become champions and do so every year. When presented with a poor lot of competitors, the judge has the right to withhold winners' ribbons, but this rarely happens. He does not consciously seek enemies.

In accordance with the laws of human nature, each judge interprets the standard in his own way. Short coupling, for example, is a must in our breed. Yet long Labradors reminiscent of oversized Dachshunds have been winners in the ring. The Lab standard calls for any solid-colored coat, although a "small white spot on the chest" is permissible. Some judges feel that a small spot is no larger than a quarter. Others have demonstrated that a small spot is really a dinner plate. Thus, owners of Dachshund type or dinner-plate Labs select their judges with the utmost care. So it goes in all breeds.

In the beginning, or as babes in the woods, it was our understanding that all judges read and understood the English language. This innocence was dispelled in short order. We had expected to find a wide variety of personalities (calm or nervous, courteous or rude, agreeable or cold) and did, but we did not anticipate the wide variety of interpretations. While all of the Labrador judges were obviously judging by the standard, some seemed to be using the African standard for gazelles.

Westminster arrived, and we attended as spectators. The Lab judge was an old and dear friend of ours (a fishing and poker companion for many years), and for that reason we did not enter any dogs. Sometimes the grapevine can be nasty. The breed entry was a big one and reeking with quality. To our amazement, the judge found his winners in both sexes among the smallest candidates present. Two were imports, and all were inches under the minimum size required by the standard.

When we saw him again, he asked our opinion of his selections. "They were all great dogs," he assured us, "and my decisions were difficult to make. Best of Breed, for example. I could have given it to any one of five dogs and felt I was making an honest choice."

It seemed the opportune moment, so we asked, "Then why did you settle for the undersized one?"

"What do you mean? He wasn't undersized according to the British standard! I've always said American Labs are too big."

In several breeds, including ours, the British standard differs from the American, in that it calls for a smaller height at the shoulders (usually a couple of inches). Had some fanciers known the judge's view, they would have kept their dogs at home. Our friend the judge is still active, now judges many more breeds, and the end result may be miniature everythings.

After that, we started keeping a little black book or a record of judges. Only then—as when one has an unusual operation and then discovers that fifty of his acquaintances have already undergone it—did we discover that half the dog fanciers in the land were doing the same thing. It's a wise little book for any fancier, since it saves time, money, travel, and personal feelings.

The little black book has two sections for judges, "Approved" and "Disapproved," both with appropriate remarks. Under "Approved" are the names of judges whom we feel stick close or reasonably close to the Lab standard. We may have shown under him and won or lost. We may have observed him judging Labs or other sporting breeds. Finally, we may never have seen the judge in action, but have followed his show records.* This last is a bit tricky, for one must also know most of the dogs shown under him. Thus:

Judge Hondu, 8/16/61, Troy show. Insists on loose lead, puts emphasis on movement. Knows breed.

Judge Hundu, 7/29/67. Westport show. New, California, likes them big. Winners all pros. Try again with Duke.

Judge Handu, 5/30/68, Walden show. Tricky, used bracelets to test steadiness. Conformation over movement, but loose lead.

---

* *Pure-Bred Dogs* carries complete results of all the point shows.

Judge Hindu, 6/28/65, Greenlawn show. Heads, tails, and angulation. No baiting. Open class only.

Experience or observation wins a judge's place under "Disapproved":

Judge Blank, 7/15/68, High Valley show. A nut. Advised all handlers that dogs would not be required to stand. "Too much standing results in hip dysplasia." Her BOB a dreadful pup. Told pro handler, "I loved him at four weeks and couldn't wait to see him again. Give Alice my best." Never bred or owned Labs.

Judge Blink, 9/23/65, Bellows show. Breeds Pointers, believes Labs are Pointers.

Judge Blonk, 4/16/64, Holyoke show. Very inconsistent. Likes them tall, short, long, snipey, anything goes.

Judge Blunk, 5/20/68, Springfield show. Fast, hardly looked at dogs, more interested in talking to blonde at ringside.

Judge Blutt, 8/16/67, Webster show. Forget. Senile.

Within the fancy, judges are discussed far more frequently than other fanciers, professional handlers, dogs, or the weather. All judges are aware of this, but none have a defense against gossip and rumors. Even mother love, that sacred American institution, comes under attack in the dog fancy.

Savage, must-win fanciers may disagree, but all judges do have mothers. From time to time, some mothers have been known to enjoy dog shows and sit at ringside to watch a son or daughter render decisions. Courteous fanciers have been known to approach such mothers and pass the time of day. This innocent gesture is always misconstrued. "Be nice to his mother," the grapevine reports, "and your dog is sure to win."

Perhaps because they know it's hopeless to try to please everyone, some judges travel to a show with fanciers or handlers who will show dogs under them, or party the night before with owners, or even become a house guest of a noted fancier. All these actions are considered unethical by sensitive judges, but entirely ethical by the judges who don't give a damn. It's difficult to prove that a judge favors a dog because of the dog's owner.

A fine example was provided by a foreign judge who flew thousands of miles to reach a certain show and judge Best in Show. For several weeks, she was the house guest of a dear friend, a wealthy dog fancier. The big climax of the show came when the judge awarded Best in Show to her host's dog. The grapevine's hot lines worked overtime for the next few days.

If judges won't protect themselves,* the fancy is trying to do so at the kennel-club level. Each year, a few more clubs rule that their own officers cannot show dogs at their own point shows. The officers, of course, hire the judges, often entertain them the night before a show, and sometimes shelter them as house guests.

It's a fine idea, certainly better than nothing, but not guaranteed to work. What happens when the club president's dog goes Best in Show a week later at another show and under the judge who had been the president's house guest?

Overall, judges are obviously more important to professional handlers than to the amateur fanciers. For that reason, one would think that every professional would defend the reputation of every judge to the death. Not so.

It's a rare point show when at least one ambitious pro doesn't take a novice fancier aside and confide, "I was watching you in the ring, and I could tell Judge Plotch liked your dog, but he doesn't know you. He'll be judging again at Syracuse in a couple of weeks, so why don't you let me handle your dog for you? He owes me a win." This conversational ploy has its variations, but all imply that Plotch, who might be the treasurer of General Motors, is a scoundrel in his avocation: to insure the loyalty of the professionals who keep entering big numbers of dogs under him, Plotch rotates his wins among them.

If the newcomer is eager to win at any cost, the plot works. Next time out, the dog wins or loses under Plotch. If the dog wins,

* Judicial naïveté is not permitted above the border, where the Canadian Kennel Club spanks any of its socializing judges.

the newcomer is sure the dog game is crooked, and the handler has another client. If the dog loses, the handler reports, "Plotch really loved your dog, but he couldn't give him the win because Ethel Throttle was there with a new dog, and Ethel [another professional] gave Plotch a piano last Christmas." Now the novice fancier is really sure that the dog game is just a branch of the Mafia. If he can't afford to give away pianos, he quits the game and spreads the word that judges and professionals have a racket going for them.

Less common is an outright attack by the professionals on a judge. One of the memorable cases concerned professional Harry Gool of Doberman Pinscher fame. He was also an importer and breeder, and he knew as much about a Dobie as any living man. Indeed, the fancy agreed that the breed's two top authorities were Harry and Judge Ringo. The judge was also famous as a drinking man of the old school.

For some twenty years, Harry's breeding program produced some of the best Dobies in the world. And then he came up with a dog whom he considered to be the perfect Dobie. A wealthy fancier agreed, bought the dog for a record figure, and started campaigning him. Harry was the handler, of course. The dog set a fast pace. He went undefeated in his breed, won many groups, and went on to several Best in Shows.

Finally, at one of the nation's biggest shows, the dog went under Judge Ringo for the first time. And for the first time, the mighty Dobie failed to take the breed. His victor was never heard from again. Harry's dog continued his winning ways.

But Harry didn't forget Ringo. He waited two years for his moment of vengeance, and it came at a large indoor shows as he and a bevy of handlers watched Ringo at work in the Whippet ring. As he was gaiting the Novice class of dogs, the judge started to cross the ring in the manner of a sailor walking the deck of a boat plowing through heavy seas. Ringo stumbled and fell. He was helped to his feet and the judging continued.

The night before, the handlers had been present at a party tossed by the show's sponsoring kennel club. Ringo had been roaring drunk, a not unusual state for him. The handlers were pretty sure that he had followed his usual practice of enjoying a late, liquid breakfast.

Now Harry filed charges against Ringo with the A.K.C., claiming that Ringo had judged while under the influence of alcohol and naming the other handlers as witnesses. In due time, Harry, Ringo, and the handlers were assembled for a formal hearing on the matter. Almost to a man, Harry and the other handlers offered their damaging testimony. Ringo, of course, had to sit through the ordeal.

His one bright moment came when the final handler testified: "I was not at the party, I did not see the judge at breakfast, but I did see him stumble and fall in the ring. It so happens that I took a Whippet dog into the Open class. I noticed nothing peculiar about the judging. I was close to Judge Ringo and did not scent liquor on his breath. But I am a handler and not a medical man."

Otherwise, the evidence against Ringo was overwhelming, and his judging license was suspended. Later, he applied for reinstatement, and within a year he was judging again.

Harry never showed under Ringo again, and he still doesn't talk to the nonmedical handler. Ringo now peers down on all dog shows from that part of heaven reserved for dog-show judges.

"I miss him," the handler who didn't condemn the judge confided. "Ringo was an honest judge. I handled dogs under him many times in his last years, and they won usually. I think he knew more about Whippets than any judge who ever lived."

Do professionals keep little black books? The smart ones do. Do judges keep them? Who knows?

We've often thought of publishing and selling little black books. It may be the best way for amateurs to make money in the dog game.

CHAPTER V

EASY TRAINING

THE SHOW dog must know how to gait and stand properly. The gait is always a trot and never a pace. The stance may or may not be his natural one, but it is the one that shows off his conformation to the best advantage.

Classes in handling for the breed ring are held all over the country. Most match shows hold such classes before the judging begins. Many kennel clubs and dog organizations offer evening classes as a regular part of their programs. But, though they are useful for the new fancier, remember that all breeds are not handled in the same way. Thus a teacher experienced in the art of handling Bulldogs might not know a damn thing about Vizslas. A student, then, would be wise to check and find out if a member of the teaching staff is familiar with his particular breed.

The schools, the textbooks, most fanciers, and most professionals pay primary attention to gaiting. Once the dog has that down pat, he is then taught, if need be, to stand properly. Often, but not always, a well-balanced dog's natural stance is the right one.

Traditionally then, gaiting is taught first and then stance. We held hands with this tradition for many years, and then decided to practice it in reverse. Ever since, we've been antitraditionalists, in that stance is perfected before gaiting.

This has worked to our advantage many times in the breed ring. Consider the pattern of judging:

First, all the dogs in competition gait in a circle around the ring. The judge is getting his first impression of each dog's movement. A sort of side impression.

Next, the dogs are halted in line and stand for the judge's inspection. If a dog is not in proper stance, there's plenty of time for the handler to make corrections. He does this by moving the dog's legs until he stands just right. In an average class, half the handlers do just that. The judge, then, sees every dog in perfect stance. If there's any doubt in his mind, he might lift a dog's front leg and drop it. The leg might not drop straight from the shoulder, or the paw might not fall in line. Too bad. If the judge continues with the rear legs, a fine hock might become a cow hock.

Eventually, the judge has each dog gaited individually. The dog is moved away from him and then back to him, so that he can study movement from both rear and front. On the final few steps of the return, the dog is brought to a halt before the judge. In that instant, the handler has no time to correct his dog. In effect, the dog is on his own. If he's standing all over the place, or if his front appears to be that of Charlie Chaplin below the waist, the judge cannot be favorably impressed.

Sometimes, when a judge cannot make up his mind between two dogs, he has them gaited again, either individually or together. He considers them equal in conformation and movement, and he is looking for something that will mean the difference between them. The difference is often apparent in the final view, that last instant when the dogs halt before him. A sloppy stance won't take home the win.

So we put the first emphasis on stance. It is so important, so much of a convincer, that we know that our dogs have often scored wins over others that were really superior specimens of the breed because of stance.

Usually, the training begins when the dog is a pup and as time permits. From two to seven months, a pup's fastest growing period, he goes through one awkward stage after another. His parts seem to mature at individual rates, and often his legs insist on acting independently.

When he's about three months old, we start setting him up. We begin informally, and the lessons last no more than three or four minutes twice a day. He is required to stand still and hold his head up. How he stands is unimportant.

The only command words used are "stand" (for his whole body) and "up" (for his head), the latter with a little pat under the chin. At first, all this seems like nonsense to the pup. He's full of fun, not used to using his brain, and prefers action. A frisky pup will try the teacher's patience for a couple of days, but he learns the command words in a few days and responds to flattery and petting. The lessons are always held in a room or a corner of the yard that's void of distractions, such as other dogs, romping children, and inventions any pup wants to investigate.

On the fourth or fifth day, each lesson is scheduled just prior to his meal. Now the meal becomes his reward for standing still. This system continues into the second week, or until he stands reasonably still before the teacher, who holds the meal pan in his hands. At this point, "stand" is the only verbal command needed. His head will be up, watching that pan. If he barks, that's fine. He still considers the training to be a game, and he'll forget about making noise long before he enters the show ring.

Now the pup is getting three meals a day. For the next couple of weeks, he is required to stand still before every meal. Sixty seconds is long enough. Then he is praised and fed.

The formal part of the training begins early in his fourth month. We call it the crate method, for we use a metal crate. A rubber tread has been glued to the top of the crate to provide firm footing. Actually, a crate isn't necessary. A wooden box, table, or bench can also be used, so long as it stands firmly and doesn't have a slippery top surface.

The pup is placed on the crate and told to stand there. Now he begins to learn about proper show stance. If the pup doesn't do so himself, the teacher places the two forelegs in the proper posi-

Thumper of Walden (then 11 months) demonstrates the Crate Method under the critical eye of his owner-handler, our daughter Cary. Dog breezed to his championship. *Kammet*

tion. Up off the ground, the pup doesn't feel too secure and he's not likely to move his position.

One daily session is enough for any pup. Timing isn't important, and we don't plan it before a meal unless it's convenient. However, the canine student always gets a reward for his efforts: a couple of pieces of kibble are sufficient. And once he knows where his forelegs should be planted, he starts learning about his hindlegs.

For almost all breeds, the proper show stance is pretty much the same, and calls for a straight front. The forelegs fall to the ground on a straight line from the shoulders, and they are always an equal distance apart. The paws point straight ahead. From the side, the forelegs appear to stand at right angles to the ground.

Butch, the Samoyed who thought he was a Labrador, demonstrates proper stance after graduating from crate to ground. Evie is checking the dog's front a few hours before a breed judge did likewise and made him a champion. *Kammet*

If the above is not the case, then the pup is not holding his elbows close and is practicing a misdemeanor known as elbows out. Correct by grasping the elbow, lifting the leg, and placing it down properly. Or, if the pup is not one of the big breeds, place one hand under his brisket, lift him, and drop him. If he doesn't fall true, then it's back to the elbows.

The above does not apply to such breeds as the Bulldog, Basset Hound, Pekingese, and Corgi. In a sense, nature edited the standards for those breeds, and man hasn't been able to change them.

Once the pup learns to stand correctly up front for a few minutes—usually a matter of less than a week—attention is paid to his rear and topline. While there is more variance in the hind legs of the breeds, most call for a little more setback and more spread than up front. The hocks are the things to watch. They should be fairly straight and at right angles to the ground. Correct by grasping hock, lifting and repositioning leg.

Topline should be straight and level in most breeds. Correct by lifting under the belly. A good test of a properly positioned rear is to apply a bit of hand pressure on top of the rump. If the pup stays steady, then he's right.

Unless the pup is stupid, he should be standing properly about the end of the second week. An adult dog should learn in one week. With a pup, we use the crate method for about a month, and we don't worry about missing a day or two. After a few days, any pup grasps the reason for being up on the crate, and he becomes more cooperative. We have found that the method has its fringe benefits. For our breed, it's an ideal height for grooming a dog and trimming his nails.

A final word of caution: study your breed standard for the precise details of your breed's show stance. Setters and German Shepherd Dogs are required to present a sloping topline. Sporting dogs require more angulation (stifle) than Terriers. But whatever the requirements, we believe that they can be taught best on the top of a crate.

Now, when the pup knows how to stand, we turn to gaiting. This is done on lead, of course, and by this time he's already accustomed to collar and lead.

Volumes have been written about training a dog to collar and lead, and most of it has been a bunch of rubbish. When a pup is about ten weeks old, we slip a collar around his neck, attach a lead to the collar, and take him for a ten-minute walk. Sometimes he picks the direction, and sometimes we do. We lead or he leads. Walking in the woods is fine. In a strange place, the pup is a little unsure and tends to stay close. If we must go from A to B (as in crossing a street) and he objects, we lift and carry him to B. The pup's feelings are never hurt.

To the pup, walking on lead is just another game for the first few days. Then he starts hearing the word "Heel" for the first time, and learns to walk at his teacher's left side. Whenever he decides to wander, he hears the command "Heel" and feels a sudden pull on his neck. A slight jerk on the lead provides the pull. After a very few sessions, the pup's natural instinct for preservation tells him that he won't feel the sudden pull if he stays at his teacher's side. Praise and a tidbit are always the rewards for good performance.

The breed-ring gait for every breed is a trot, but some pups and some dogs don't know this, nor do their handlers. They think a pace is a trot. Fine for a camel, but not for a show dog. Canine anatomy is not designed for pacing, so the pacing dog doesn't do justice to his moving parts. Correct a pacing dog by halting him, then starting up again. For the uninformed, pacing amounts to both legs on one side moving in unison.

In the ring, the dog is required to gait in two ways and sometimes three. Always, he must gait in an anticlockwise, big circle, and also away from and back to the judge. For home training, a rock, post, or tree can substitute for a judge, although a living person is desirable.

Not every judge requires the third gaiting maneuver, but those who do will describe it to the first handler and his dog and then hope that the other handlers will follow suit. Ten dull handlers, however, will require ten sets of instructions and make the judge unhappy. The average judge, hoping for the best, is very explicit and points for emphasis: "Gait your dog to the right corner, then

to the left corner, then back to the right corner, then back to me."
If the dog is properly handled, the judge's eagle eyes study the
candidate's action from the rear, both sides, and the front.

This pattern throws many a novice handler and his charge into
a tizzy, so it's best to work out the pattern on the home grounds.
If the handler comes between the dog and the judge, the judge's
view is obstructed. With the dog at the handler's left, all goes well
on the trip to the right corner and on to the left corner. There
the handler must switch the lead to his right hand, journey back
to the right corner, and then head back to the judge. All this calls
for some twisting and turning on the part of handler and dog, for
the dog does not halt until he gets back to the judge. After a few
practice sessions, the dog is no longer confused. After a few more,
the handler gets the hang of it.

In early practice sessions, we bring the pup to a halt before a
substitute judge by saying "Whoa" and tugging back simultaneously on the lead. The pup takes three or four steps before
stopping in, ideally, perfect stance. Hands shouldn't be used to
make a correction at this point. If the stance is not right, leading
the pup a step or two more usually adjusts it.

The gaiting sessions do not have to be held on a daily basis. A
couple of times a week are enough, and there's still plenty of time
before he's six months old and eligible for his first point show.
Some match shows, however, have puppy classes in the three-to-
six-months bracket.

Here are some other training tactics that we have employed
successfully with our dogs and aren't likely to abandon:

Gaiting. It's important to adjust to the dog's rate of speed.
The handler walks while a small breed trots. The handler walks
fast or may trot himself with the medium-sized and big breeds.
With a German Shepherd Dog, the handler may have to run.

So the handler must discover the dog's best gait, the one portray-
ing canine locomotion at its finest, and adjust to it. Following an
experienced professional handler from ring to ring at a given point
show makes an instructive day for anyone. As he handles different

breeds in different sizes, he adjusts his own speed to suit the individual dog.

Of course, this sort of study can lead to disaster. Over the last decade, one of the top professionals has been a woman with an infallible sense for gaiting. She has developed her own style, and is never seen running or trotting. It is something in between, and we think of it as loping. Whatever it may be, the style is graceful, she can slow or accelerate it, and it seems to float her along with heels kicking in the air. In her case, we suppose the lope came about quite naturally, and it has certainly contributed to her success. Well, the younger generation has studied her—superficially at least. These days, almost any point show has its compliment of teen-age girl handlers bouncing around the breed rings in their interpretations of their idol's lope. Watching them is a splendid spectator sport. Some kick out so severely that they seem to ram their own posteriors, which may help propel them. The unnatural lopes do not appear to help the dogs.

Stance. In the ring, only foolish handlers take their eyes off their dogs for more than a second. Unlike humans, the canine has a mysterious power that enables him to shift weight without flexing a muscle or moving his legs.

Look at the dog. His stance is perfect!

Steal a glance at the judge to see what he's doing.

Look at the dog again. By God, his back is curved! How did that happen? Or his forelegs are leaning forward or back.

If a slap on the side doesn't take out the curve, wheel him around and reposition him. If a rap on the chest doesn't correct a forward lean, reposition the legs. If he's leaning back, pull on the tail a bit, then release. He usually swings ahead. If not, reposition the legs.

At outdoor shows, uneven ground often prevents the best-trained dog from achieving a balanced stance. A wise handler keeps his eye peeled for ground depressions and slopes. Moving a dog a few feet out of line to find even territory doesn't call for a penalty.

In all Groups except Sporting, dogs stay on lead when standing for the judge's inspection. Traditionally, that is. For reasons never explained, the tradition isn't always followed with Sporting breeds these days, and some judges permit the lead to remain. In some circles, including ours, this new trend is regarded as unfortunate. A tight lead holds the dog's head up (he hates to strangle) and also helps camouflage loose shoulders. This doesn't fool a wise judge, but wisdom varies in any social set.

Collar and Lead. On the home grounds, for both pups and adult dogs, we use the plain cotton-nylon slip collar. This is also used for training, although a particularly rambunctious pup might wear a small linked-chain choke collar. When extended to maximum size, either collar just fits over the ears and hangs loosely around the dog's neck.

There's no need for a big, strong, wide collar on any dog, regardless of age—if he's had any training and hasn't reverted to the wild state. And for the show dog, coat must be considered: a heavy collar, leather or chain, will break down the hairs and may also stain them.

Except for showing, the practical lead to use at all times is the ordinary canvas work lead. It's cheap, durable, washable, comes in a variety of widths and lengths, and simply snaps onto the collar ring.

For almost all of the breeds, the best collar and lead for the show ring is known as the show lead. This has an adjustable loop for use as a collar. The lead is never more than a half inch in width, runs some thirty inches in length, comes in a variety of colors and costs about two dollars. They are sold at shows and at most pet shops. These leads are easy to remove and put back on in the ring (Sporting breeds) and any excess can be rolled into the palm of one's hand when gaiting the dog.

In the ring, the handler holds the lead in his left hand (except for a special gaiting situation). It is employed in one of two ways: as a tight or a loose lead.

The tight lead is an American innovation, introduced by professional handlers and since copied by many amateur fanciers. The fanciers don't always know why they are using the tight lead, but the professionals do: it can help hide some of a dog's faults.

Among other things, it corrects elbows, loose shoulders, and head position. The lead is held short and directly above a dog's head. When the lead is held very tight, a gaiting dog seems to be treading on air with his front paws. This is known as stringing up the dog, a polite term for hanging.

We happen to oppose any form of hanging in the breed ring, and agree with Tex Wright of Vermont, who has been handling his homebred Pointers in the ring for some thirty-five years: "A dog who can't hold his head up without help isn't worth a damn!"

To our regret, the very tight lead is now common in the Sporting breed rings. "Loose" means precisely what it implies: the lead dangles or loops from the handler's hand, and the dog is obviously proceeding in his normal fashion. He's strictly on his own.

Still common in England, but rapidly disappearing here, the loose lead is preferred by many judges. Unfortunately, some prefer and do not insist. We have been present several times when this sort of debate ensued between the judge and a handler:

"I said loose lead! Gait your dog again!" (Handler gaits dog on tight lead.) "Loose lead! Try again!" (Handler gaits dog and strings him up.) "Once more. And please, please, a loose lead." (Handler again strings up dog, who is now gasping for air.) "Thank you, sir. Your dog wins!"

Offhand, we can think of several Labrador judges who are also breeders and exhibitors. All insist upon a loose lead. They warn a handler once and only once. If the handler continues to use a tight lead, his dog is usually out of the running. Bravo!

Bravo thus far, that is. When said judges handle their own dogs in the ring, all string up their dogs!

Socialization. A first show, match or point, can be quite a traumatic experience for any pup or adult dog. He's never seen as many dogs in one place or scented so many strange smells, heard so many strange noises or witnessed so much confusion. Many a brave pup has tucked his tail between his legs and entered the ring as a shivering shy creature. A pup or dog without spirit might as well be left at home.

To prepare the pup for the new world, we have always used an informal program called socialization. It amounts to no more than acquainting him with new noises, people, places, and experiences. The program is designed for our convenience, not his.

At home, when we don't have headaches, this means banging down his meal pan, slamming doors, and having him handy when the lawnmower or chain saw is being used. No particular attention is paid to him. Sooner or later, he adjusts.

Once in a while, we take him on a short trip. The trip might be to the bank, or to the airport or railway station to pick somebody up. If a factory whistle blows as we pass by, we consider the noise a bonus. This travel has its fringe benefits, of course. The pup stays in a crate and gets used to that. If he's subject to car sickness (this seldom happens), he soon cures himself.

The pup is always on lead in public places, of course, and strangers, if they are so inclined, are encouraged to pet him. Usually, the judges he meets in the breed ring will be complete strangers to him. And some of these will be ladies who wear a dozen clanking bracelets on each arm—not to frighten the pup but to test his steadiness.

When friends visit and there's time to spare, we sometimes have one act the part of a judge. With the pup in show stance, he goes over the dog as every judge will: examining bite, running hands over shoulders, measuring tail, perhaps adjusting legs and applying pressure on the rump. If the pup regards this as too personal at first, he calms down and holds steady after a few such experiences.

Socialization means that the pup is with his master more of the time, and companionship is the basic reason for owning a pet anyway. It can do no harm, and it does prepare the show dog for the ring.

As a result, our dogs are sometimes better prepared than we are.

Age for Showing. This depends more on the fancier than his dog. Some can't wait for the pup to become six months old. The rational ones know the pup doesn't have the maturity to win points in competition with older dogs, although hope is eternal and lightning does strike.

When he was two, we had our Duke in the ring at a large Eastern show. He needed a major win to finish his championship and Winners Dog that day was worth four points.

Duke won his Open class and remained in the ring for the judging of Winners Dog and the four points. When the other winners were assembled, it was obvious to all watching that Duke had to be the logical choice. He was just moments away from his championship, and we wondered why the lady judge was taking so much time. She was a breeder of Labradors, newly licensed and judging in the East for the first time.

Finally, the lady pointed to the Puppy class winner, the least likely choice among the contenders. A single spectator applauded: the pup's owner. The pup's professional handler was pleased, but the expression on his face was total amazement. The four-point pup was just shy of seven months. He was all legs, sported too long a tail, had been unable to gait properly, and—with the exception of coat color—did not really resemble a Labrador. Truly a dreadful representative of the breed.

Judges do not usually explain their decisions in the ring, but this lady decided to do so. Perhaps the sea of bewildered faces inspired her. "I know this puppy doesn't look like much," she explained, "but I based my decision on his potential. A year from now, he will be a great dog!"

Unless the fancier can find that judge, or one of her ilk, the best a young pup can hope to win in the ring is experience. He may win his class, but he won't have the maturity to compete with his elders for points.

We seldom show a pup before his eleventh month, and prefer to wait until he's well over a year. Then one finds out in a hurry if the educated guess was correct.

The young pup is a boy, and he's being asked to do a man's job.

Condition. Ideally, the show pup or dog should be in hard condition. This means keeping him lean and exercised. A couple of pups in a run will play and get sufficient exercise. A couple of adults may sleep all day.

A fat, round pup is happy and belongs to a silly owner. A pup's growing bones are soft and can't stand excessive weight. Keep him fat and he'll never realize whatever his potential is supposed to be. Keep him lean, or with just enough flesh to cover the rib cage, and he'll be happy and healthy, and will mature in the right manner.

The right diet is the one that keeps him properly lean. The quantity of food per meal is a matter of visual judgment. If the pup starts packing on fat, the quantity is reduced. A weekly check is sufficient.

Unlike kittens, pups don't know when to stop eating. Thus giving him all he'll eat is always a poor idea. This is also true of adult dogs, some of whom consider eating to be their purpose on earth. Some are catholic in their tastes and dine on pebbles, pieces of wood, and anything else they find. For over ten years now, our wastebaskets have been more decorative than utilitarian. Folly, one of our house dogs, tours the rooms several times a day, hoping to find such tasty morsels as envelopes, pencil butts, and silver foil. She has never been known to refuse any food prepared for human consumption.

Travel Trouble. Our friendly veterinarian estimates that some twenty million beloved American dogs travel around on poor feet, and the blame belongs to their owners. His view is not as apocryphal as it may seem. Most owners aren't aware of the fact, but good vets always check out a dog's feet before releasing him. If the nails are long, he clips them. More often than not, the nails are long.

The average dog doesn't get enough exercise to wear down his nails. If left untrimmed, the paw becomes splayed (spread toes) and a flat-footed canine results. Then, to find the most comfortable position, the dog travels with paws turned either in or out.

Straight paws are essential for show dogs in almost all of the breeds. But even the exceptions (Bulldog, Basset Hound) require a compact paw.

Anyone capable of trimming his own fingernails will have no difficulty trimming a dog's nails. Still, some of our friends pay a vet, pet shop, or professional handler to perform the simple chore.

Their excuses range from lack of time and uncooperative dogs to personal nervousness and a tendency to faint at the sight of blood.

Aside from nervousness, the routine excuses are not valid. Trimming isn't a daily event and takes less time than journeying to the vet. There are always ways to make the most frantic dog cooperative, and blood isn't necessary.

Two pieces of equipment are available for nail trimming. One is hand-powered, a two-handled affair held in one hand. When pressure is applied to the handles, they act as levers and shoot forward a cutting edge. Time per nail is almost zero.

A bit more expensive is the electric nail trimmer. This is a handle with an extended axle and wheel. The wheel carries a replaceable sandpaper disk. Again, it is held in one hand. In effect, the nail is sanded down to the proper length. With one's free hand, of course, the dog's paw and individual toes are held steady. Time per nail is about twenty seconds.

The nail is trimmed down to just short of the vein (quick). A dog's nail should be just short of the ground. When a dog walks across a wooden or linoleum floor and a *click-click-click* sound is heard, his nails are overdue for a trimming.

Bleeding occurs when the vein is cut. One big advantage to the electric model is that it cauterizes the quick and stems the bleeding. But nail bleeding is nothing to worry about. The dog won't bleed to death, and a wad of cotton, styptic pencil or just plain running on the ground will halt the flow.

We start trimming a pup's nails at five weeks. He's not quite weaned by then, and the nails might damage his dam's belly. Up to about ten months, any pup's greatest period of growth, the nails are checked every three weeks. After ten months, the check is made four or five times a year.

The younger one starts a pup, the sooner he becomes accustomed to the painless interlude, and he develops into a cooperative creature. Canine nature is as diversified as human nature, however. Some dogs prefer to stand and others are calmest lying on one side. In those cases, the top of a crate makes an ideal trimming site. Our only oddball happens to be the gourmand bitch, Folly.

When she sees the hand trimmer, she goes down, rolls over on her back, and presents each paw in turn.

Our most difficult patient was Butch, a big Samoyed. All the sled-dog breeds are particular about their feet, and he was very particular. He would stand all day for grooming, but nail trimming turned him into a wild animal, and it was always a two-person job. Then came a hot summer's day when we were readying him for a show. As he was being groomed, he discovered an unguarded glass of gin and tonic. He sampled it, and then almost begged to have his nails trimmed. So there really is a way to calm every dog and we never had trouble with Butch again.

If nails* are not trimmed, their veins tend to grow longer with the years, and the day comes when they can't be trimmed short enough. Then it's good-bye to good feet.

Baiting. This is the art practiced by professional handlers and many fanciers to trick their dogs into showing themselves at their alert best. It amounts to attracting the dog's attention and is employed when the judge is inspecting the dog or looking his way.

The bait can be almost anything: a tidbit of food, a key ring, snapping fingers, or a clicker. Held in the handler's free hand, it is held before and above the standing dog's head. Only canine dullards fail to respond. Most hold their heads higher, extend their necks, and bring their ears to attention. This interest and alertness is also known as expression.

Many judges place great value on expression, and some do their own baiting by whistling or uttering peculiar noises. A judge can tire himself by trying to find expression in Bloodhounds. And then there are judges who do not permit baiting, but it does not harm to try under them. The act will bring a warning, but the dog won't be penalized.

Anyone contemplating the art of baiting should practice before trying it in the ring. The first few times, the dog may jump for the bait.

The popular American bait is a small piece of cooked, dried

---

* Dewclaws are trimmed in the same manner.

beef liver. All dogs seem to love it. We prepare it at home, but it can be purchased ready-to-use at most pet shops.

Is there any guaranteed route to instant success in the dog game? One requiring an absolute minimum of training, such as hauling a dog around on a lead?

Yes, although the fancier must be selective about his breed.

In every region of the country, some of the less popular breeds are seldom and often never seen at the point shows. These breeds include the American Foxhound, English Foxhound, Harrier, Bernese Mountain Dog, Field Spaniel, Sussex Spaniel, and Clumber Spaniel. It may take some searching, but a pup of any of these breeds can be found in this country, and certainly in England.

The owner of an eligible Harrier, then, will always win more than he loses, and the dog or bitch may never lose. Thus, since competition will seldom, if ever, be present, the Harrier will go Best of Breed at fifty point shows in a row (if his owner is that ambitious). Then the owner can decorate the wall with winning ribbons, line the mantel with trophies, and boast that his dog has never been defeated in the breed. Friends, neighbors, relatives, and the boys at the office (if none are dog fanciers) will be very impressed, and the owner becomes a dog authority in those circles.

While not common, there are dog fanciers who go in for this type of success, and they seem to derive great satisfaction from it and lead long, happy lives.

The only drawback to this plan is that the dog can be shown at hundreds of shows, never be defeated in his breed, grow old and forlorn, and never become a champion. Lacking breed competition, the dog must win his points by winning his Group, and the rare breeds seldom go that far. The fewer the pups in any breed, the fewer the great ones. So achieving a championship with a rare breed is a seldom thing.

Still, championships can be won in the rare breeds. Witness a young friend of ours who fell in love with the Flat Coated Retriever breed and found the pup he wanted in England. The pup matured into a fine dog, was entered at several shows, but couldn't find any breed competition. Undaunted, the Eastern owner journeyed to the Midwest, where the Flat Coats were enjoying a revival. The dog picked up a bundle of championship points, but he still lacked his two major wins. Unable to continue the long-distance travel, our friend kept on showing closer to home and eventually picked up two Group wins for the dog's championship.

An easier, surer, but more expensive way to turn a rare-breed dog into a champion is currently being exploited by ardent lovers of the Clumber Spaniel. The secret of success: (1) buy a dog and bitch and breed them, (2) save three male pups, or three bitch pups, and (3) start showing the male pups and the sire, or the bitch pups and the dam. For a three point (major) win in Clumbers, one sex requires four dogs in competition. Thus, show four males at enough shows and one must become a champion.

Regardless of puppy sexes, a litter of eight pups and their parents will eventually produce seven champions. All can be poor Clumbers, and they can pick up their basic training in the show ring, so long as they can be coaxed to move on lead.

This course is recommended for anyone who owns everything but a champion dog, and only two handlers are required. As with the dogs, the handlers require an absolute minimum of talent. Holding one end of a lead and walking are the only requirements. The ideal road to a specialized sort of success in the dog game for the small family. The end result, if the breeder boasts enough in the right corner, is instant fame. LOCAL MAN WINS GOLD MEDAL will be the Swamp City *Herald*'s headline. And what a wonderful story to cut and mail to envious friends: "The annual State Chamber of Commerce Gold Medal for Unusual Achievement has been awarded to Raymond K. Dingle, of Swamp City. Mr. Dingle, a local mechanic and well-known dog authority . . ."

Our friend the psychiatrist claims that breeding and showing one of the rare breeds is the perfect solution for all introverts and depressives. He thinks it's a pity that Nietzsche wasn't a dog fancier. "Take his line 'The thought of suicide is a great consolation: by means of it, one gets successfully through many a bad night.' Now then, if he had changed the beginning to 'The thought of owning a champion dog . . .' it would have more therapeutic value today."

And then there was the elder Dumas. He didn't give a damn about dogs, but he used to say that nothing succeeds like success. That fits the dog fancy today.

CHAPTER VI

BREED RING:
TIPS FROM THE TOP

Advice, Tips, Theories, Methods, and other incidentals from several of America's outstanding Fanciers: Aennchen Antonelli and Walter Goodman, Glenna Crafts and Maurie Prager § Also Additional observations from professional Handlers: Isabella Hoopes, First Woman Pro, Lloyd Case, Handler for the Duke and Duchess of Windsor § The Right Hands

AND NOTHING succeeds like experience. It doesn't always seem that way, however. Every fancier has his ups and downs, and there are times when he wonders if he's forgotten all that he's learned. Then his dog starts winning, and he knows twice as much as he ever did.

While there's no rule of thumb for success in the dog game, the solid success stories seldom happen overnight. They concern the dog game's hard core, those amateurs who haven't made dogs their life, but wouldn't think of living life over again without dogs. Almost all of them drifted into the dog game with one or two dogs. All became entranced, and ended up as breeders. All of them continued to train and handle their own dogs, and—in their own breeds—can give the professional handlers a run for their money any day in the week. Of the amateurs seen in the Best in Show ring, they are the ones seen most frequently. Many times, the judge rendering the high decision knows less about their breed than they do.

When one of the top amateurs is in the ring, the practice of handling takes on a new dimension. All of the professionals present know that their bonus money is threatened, and all the tricks are pulled out of each handler's private book. It is ring warfare at its best.

In any section of the country, there's seldom more than one highly rated amateur per breed. When there are two, they are usually man and wife. In every case, a wise line breeding program has paid off and is producing dogs of unusual quality, and the fancier has devoted long hours to care and training. Intelligence, not luck, is the key to substantial success, also defined as the breeding and handling of top dogs.

Every handler, professional or amateur, develops his own training methods over the years. The methods are regarded as trade secrets, although hundreds of other handlers may have been doing the same things for decades and not broadcasting the news. Nevertheless, each handler feels his system gives him an edge over all other handlers.

He is always modest about his secrets. When Mary Smith handled her Great Dane, the dog gaited at an angle and always headed in on her. She hired professional Alex Zop, and two weeks later he had the dog gaiting straight and true. "Nothing to it," Alex explained to Mary. "I was just a little firm with him." Trade secret? Whenever the dog headed in on Alex, he brought up his left knee and banged it against the dog's head. After three days of that, the dog gaited straight and Alex had a sore knee. The dog didn't like Alex, but the man had a new client.

Often, a trade secret is logical. Quite often, it is a theory, and theories in the dog game run pretty wild.

A Boston Terrier fancier: "We do not show outdoors on fair days. Bostons are more spirited when it is overcast."

Lhasa Apso breeder: "Let's say the dog is to be shown on Saturday. I give him hell on Tuesday and Wednesday. I don't speak to him at all on Thursday and Friday. He sulks. On Saturday, about an hour before ring time, I tell him I love him. His spirits soar and he shows magnificently."

A Yorkshire Terrier owner: "He doesn't show well under tall judges, and that's always seemed odd to me. His dam liked them tall. I never knew his sire."

Our favorite theorist happens to be a Labrador man, whose show dogs are usually yellow. In the ring, the dogs always appear to have enjoyed recent mud baths. Judges, of course, are not too fond of dogs wearing filthy coats.

One day, at a large outdoor show, we noted our fellow Lab lover walking along with two of his muddy dogs on leads. We assumed that the dogs had broken loose and cavorted in a nearby swamp. Since breed judging was only minutes away, we offered to help clean the dogs. "No, thank you!" was the fancier's response. "I want the judge to know that my dogs are used for hunting. The mud will tell him that the dogs are just out from under the gun." After about three years of showing muddy dogs, the fancier dropped out of the dog game, convinced that all judges are crooked.

The impractical secrets are a dime a dozen, or can be harvested without charge at any dog show. Bridging the moats to the practical secrets—the time-tested-and-tried hints and tips—is something else again. Most of our top amateurs aren't about to reveal anything, or are saving everything for books they will never write. But a few are willing to talk, and to reveal some of the things they've learned along the the way in the dog game. Their hope is that their own experiences will be helpful to newcomers and veterans alike. We, of course, are also looking for an edge.

One of the land's best-known amateur handlers is historian Walter Goodman, a man who knew successful careers as actor, television producer, banker, and business executive before devoting himself to what happened in the years that used to be. Dogs have been his avocation for a long time, or since 1935, when his parents gifted him with his first pet dog, a Skye Terrier. Walter fell in love with the breed, and stayed with it right down to the present, and shows no signs of ever deserting it. His accomplishments in the dog game have inspired rumors that he invented the Skye breed. Not true. Walter was born in this country, not Scotland, and more recently than 1560.

In 1969, the good news for all amateurs in the dog game was that one of their own, Walter Goodman, had handled his home-bred Ch. Glamoor Good News to Best in Show at prestigious Westminster. She was the first Skye ever to top that show, and Walter was only the third amateur in forty years to be on the other end of the Westminster winner's leash. It was a remarkable victory for an amateur, and so disturbed the professionals that a few contemplated suing him for defamation of character. Most professionals are willing to grant a few important wins to amateurs every year, but Westminster is their sacred ground. The bonus gravy is great.

Walter is a seasoned BIS winner. He's handled dogs to that honor more times than most professionals, even though the latter enter far more shows with many more dogs of different breeds. Ever since 1950, when their Ch. High Times Miss Gesty was the first Skye ever to go BIS, he and his mother have been enthusiastic breeders and exhibitors. But that first great dog of theirs was handled by a professional. Since 1955, Walter has done all the handling, and a look at his record in just recent years is most impressive. He piloted Ch. Jacinthe de Ricelaine to thirty-five BISs, a world record for the breed. Her daughter is Ch. Glamoor Good News, and Good News's litter brother is Ch. Go Go Go, and either of those dogs, if the Goodmans really cared to campaign them, could break Jacinthe's record. They are both well known BIS dogs.

How did the handler of all three feel about the big win at Westminster? "I was hoping, of course," Walter remembered. "The judge walked straight toward us. He glanced at one other dog, and I held my breath. But he kept coming and I knew we had it. First I was happy, then numb, and then I fell apart at the seams. By God, I've never felt so tired."

So, for the millions who dream of winning Westminster and never will, that's how it feels. Tired. Nobody knows how the BIS dog feels.

Ch. Glamoor Good News, top dog at Westminster 1969. *William P. Gilbert*

The Goodmans are positive proof that a great kennel can be pint-sized. They never run to more than seven or eight adult dogs, and three or four of those are usually oldsters and retired from the dog game. They like to have a couple of dogs for showing and at least one replacement coming along. All the dogs are house dogs, but seldom at the same time. A small kennel room is within the house for bitches in heat or rambunctious youngsters. "It's purposely small," according to Walter. "Otherwise, we'd be flooded with dogs we want to keep."

He has no particular strategy for showing, except for cutting it to a minimum during the summer months. In other seasons, he enters at shows near and far, when its convenient and without special concern for the judges. "Of course, if a judge doesn't give my dog a look at six straight shows, I don't hurry to go under him again. It takes me a while, but I get the message."

We'll take his word, but we doubt that there are such judges in the land. The newest of breed judges, the ones who might not recognize the handler, would certainly know that Goodman's dog deserved a good look. Few judges know as much about the breed as he does; he exhibits only the best specimens and presents them in sound and immaculate condition. He loves them all but shows only his best, and thus enters the breed ring as a pretty confident man.

Watching Walter in action, one would think that he has found the answer to almost every amateur's curse: nervousness. If all one hears and reads is correct, then the handler's jitters run down the lead to his dog and affects the dog. In Goodman's case, looks are deceiving. "I'm tense as hell in the breed ring," he admits. Still, his Skye looks as calm as the waters of a small pond on a windless day. Maybe the five-to-six-inch coat hides the tenseness. "If we take the breed and move along to Group, the tenseness lowers. Then, God and the judge willing, if we take the Group and move into the BIS ring, my pulse is close to normal." So as his fortunes increase on the day, his nerves settle. This is in direct contrast to the norm for an amateur, but Walter has never consulted a doctor.

He's also contrary to the norm when it comes to campaigning a dog. Almost any handler, amateur or pro, will exhibit a winning dog at show after show after show, pushing his luck in the manner of a gambler in a hot streak at Monte Carlo. Great as the dog may be, boredom or weariness will get to him, and then a beast of lesser quality and more spirit will take him to the cleaners. A Goodman dog is well rested and fresh when he trots into the ring, and always shows at his best. Keeping a dog fresh is hardly a problem for Walter, since he always keeps a couple of dogs going, and the Saturday one is seldom the Sunday one.

The successful handlers all have their pet theories about training their potential show pups, and all the theories seem to work, even when in conflict. With an eye to the strangers (judges) in their future who will run hands over their bodies, Walter invites the neighborhood children to play with his pups. No mauling, no rough stuff, but the use of hands is requested on all parts of the pup's body. The pup also visits the big city, with its confusion of sights, sounds, and smells. The net result is a nonshy animal who can take the dog-show din and adventures in stride.

Owner-handler Walter Goodman and Good News are interviewed by the press moments after the Skye took Terrier Group. Hours later, Walter lugged his charge back to the Best in Show ring and won all the loot. *The New York Times*

The Skye Terrier breed doesn't move up very much in popularity standings, and now ranks around seventieth. That long outer coat discourages a great many potential owners who favor the breed but not the grooming. It's all an illusion. So long as the Skye doesn't run in the mud or through thickets, the grooming is easy—once a month for the pet dog, and every two or three weeks for the show dog. Walter may add the finishing touches at a show, or arrive early enough to do the complete job. He thinks diet is important for the right-textured coat, and that both protein and oils are important. At Glamoor, an adult Skye's daily meal consists of a half pound of ground beef and about three cups of small kibble, plus one egg and cooked vegetables. A boiled egg is usual among canine feeders, but Walter prefers to feed a scrambled egg to his canine charges, with a glob of butter and a little milk added. All that keeps a thirty-pound Skye's coat and body in condition.

Here at Walden, just in case any Skye Terriers are interested, a sixty-pound Lab stays in condition on four cups of kibble per meal, plus meat or fish, an egg twice a week, plus bacon grease (when we have it), peanut oil, or suet every other day. The kibble soaks in well water (since we have a well) for fifteen minutes, then a quarter can of dog meat or canned mackerel (we prefer mackerel, since fish has more protein than meat, plus oils for coat) is added and mixed. The eggs are hard boiled, and they are always duck eggs (since we have ducks). Cooked vegetables do not add weight, but we add them to make a meal look bigger and fool a gluttonous dog. We don't know why Walter feeds scrambled eggs, but it is not a matter of personal taste. He prefers a shirred egg.

There's a new litter at Glamoor about every eighteen months. Walter's educated guess comes when the pups are ten weeks old, but he leaves ample time to change his mind: none of the pups is sold until they reach five months. By then, he's sure just which pups will be his future show and breeding prospects. He holds on to one or two.

Of all the top amateurs, he's the most casual about training. Sooner or later, or as time permits, the pup is introduced to collar, lead, and gaiting. After the pup has his gaiting on lead down pat, Walter pays attention to that other basic of breed ring: proper stance. "I really teach patience and not stance" is the way the Skye man puts it. "The right conformation means balance, and balance means the dog will stand pretty close to correctly, even as a pup. My only problem with a pup is getting him to stand quietly for two or three minutes. I just talk to him, and scold him if he moves. At six months, a Skye pup will stand and listen attentively to 'Let's talk of graves, of worms, or epitaphs,' et cetera, from Act Three, Scene Two of King Richard the Second."

Walter doesn't rush a young pup into the breed ring. He figures ten months is early enough and often waits longer, just to be reasonably sure that the coat texture will be the right one.

Aennchen Antonelli

When a new Glamoor Skye appears for the first time, the professionals wince. Will this one rob them of some bread and butter? Almost always, the answer is yes.

The breed Goodman has made famous,* or vice versa, is low and long, but a giant compared to the five-pound bundle known as the Maltese. Anyone who doesn't think that good things come in small packages will find plenty to argue about with the Toy breed's major advocates in the country, Aennchen and Tony Antonelli. Until she suffered a serious back injury, they were a popular team in the big time of the dance world, without much interest in dogs or any time for them.

Her doctors knew that Aennchen wouldn't dance again and doubted that she'd ever walk. She was tempted to hit husband Tony over the head with his welcome-home gift for her: Lover, a Maltese pup. Just taking care of the pup forced her to stumble

---

* Made famous again, really. The Skye was very popular as a pet and show dog in the Gay Nineties. Then other Terrier breeds came to the fore.

around the house, and within three weeks she was walking. The doctors were amazed, and only Tony got the message. He hustled around and bought three more pups.

So that's how the strain known as Aennchen Maltese Dancers came into being. Aennchen and Tony became breeders, of course, and as of now dogs of their breeding have won some seventy Best in Shows. Thirty-eight of that grand total were won by Ch. Aennchen's Poona Dancer, a world record for the breed. Today, their pups are found all over the dog-loving world. Yet they've never shipped a single one; a fancier intent on buying one must visit the kennel.

Aennchen does the training and handling, and she believes in a very early start. "Grooming begins as early as three and a half weeks, or as soon as the puppy can stand. Be sure to have a non-skid base on table or bench when setting up your puppy. Go through the showing experience: examine his teeth, move hands over him, talk to him, and praise him. Wear big hats and dangle jewelry. Drop pans and make odd noises. Have hulking strangers touch him. Help him become accustomed to the giantlike world around him."

She's against forcing a pup to go on lead. If he forms an early dislike, showing will never be a delight for him and he'll lack the necessary animation. Her method: "Preparing for a lead is easiest after a pup learns to follow you around and look up for a tidbit. In a few weeks, this becomes a habit for him. Then just slip a loose lead around his neck, but do it casually. He'll follow you around, looking for that reward. He doesn't know it, but he's being conditioned to do what you wish."

Preparing a Toy dog for gaiting in the breed ring calls for some precautionary training. To him, uneven ground is a battle-field and tall grass is a jungle. "Before attending outdoor shows, practice gaiting on all types of grounds," advises Aennchen. "This is of particular importance for the long-coated little fellow. His coat might catch on stubble, and if he's not used to that, his free movement will be impaired."

Once weaned, the Maltese Dancers are informally introduced to crates, find that they are friendly places, and don't suffer traumatic experiences when the time comes to be crated for a show. This won't help owners of Irish Wolfhounds, but Aennchen scatters open crates around the house and the pups consider them their homes. An Antonelli crate, better known as a vegetable bin, costs less than a dollar at a supermarket.

Aennchen considers a $2.95 door mirror to be one of her most valuable training aids. The mirror can be placed anywhere, indoors or out, and it helps in checking front and rear movement of a gaiting dog. When the dog is set up on a table, the mirror is a great help in checking on topline, front and rear. "With the mirror, work until you achieve perfection (in your own mind) with the dog, then have friends check you. Be sure they are sincere critics. You may discover that the dog is gaiting in line, but you are ruining the picture of harmony by bending over, taking too small steps, and swinging your free arm like an elephant's trunk."

Some other gleanings from the Antonelli notebook:

On the early days in the dog game: "We entered three Maltese at our first show [1954]. Two dogs and a bitch. They made a clean sweep of the breed, and we returned home on a cloud. The fact that our Maltese were the only ones at the show didn't dampen our enthusiasm. We were proud and we were hooked. Next time out, we entered only our Best of Breed dog, and he failed to win his class. A veteran breeder watched the judging, and he volunteered the information that our dog crossed in front [forelegs cross when dog moves] and would never get anywhere. We didn't know what the term meant, but our milkman did. He was a dog fancier of long standing, so we asked him to examine our dog. In his judgment, the dog did not cross in front and was a very good one. So we continued to show the dog. He became the first of the breed to win both an American and Bermudian championship, and he went on to sire twenty-eight champions. Moral: breeders met at dog shows don't always praise another breeder's dogs."

On how to succeed at showing: "It is not so much what one does in the ring as what one does before entering the ring that makes the showing experience enjoyable. If you are too busy to train your dog, don't bother showing him. Stay home and love him."

On what the handler should wear in the ring: "Clothes must

complement the dog, not detract from him. Thus, a woman handling a Dalmatian should not wear a spotted dress. As for women in general, skirts should be just full enough to permit ease for walking, kneeling, and bending. Type of material can be important. It should not show stains, dirt, and hairs. At one show, my dog's coat was full of electricity and kept flying. His hairs clung to my printed velvet suit. It was the last time I wore velvet."

On not leaving anything to chance: "Prepare a check list, itemizing the needs for your dog and yourself, and go over it before departing for a show. The collar you leave at home won't do you any good in the ring. One item that's on almost every Toy fancier's check list: give a baby suppository before leaving for show, so there won't be any accidents in the ring."

On philosophy of dog-show life: "Go!"

The one-word philosophy deserves explanation. Many fanciers with dogs entered at a given show will remain home when they learn there will not be enough dogs present in their breed to win a major in championship points. After all, winning points is the name of the game.

When Aennchen enters a dog at a show, she goes whether any other Maltese is entered or not. At the very least, she and the dog pick up some experience. On the other hand, anything can happen, including the realization of a fancier's wildest dreams.

Consider Aennchen's Sitar Dancer. The bitch puppy was the only class dog at a certain show. She went on to Best of Breed over the two Maltese champions present, but that didn't mean a thing in points. From the breed, Sitar Dancer went to Toy Group and won, and in the process picked up the major points needed to finish her championship. An hour later, the pup was acclaimed Best in Show. A rare feat, but still a little short of Smart Dancer's remarkable accomplishment. Smart Dancer, the dam of Sitar, picked up all her championship points by going from classes to three Groups and two Best in Shows. As sort of an anticlimax, she went on to six more BIS wins.

"If you've entered your dog, paid your money, and don't go, you can't win" is Aennchen's view of the dog game. Of course, if you do go, you may not win. Or if you do go and you do win,

Ch. Aennchen's Sitar Dancer, or four pounds of the dog fancier's ultimate thrill: handling a homebred from the classes to Best in Show.

your chances of turning the wild dream into a reality are about a million to one, and never realized by most fanciers in their lifetimes.

That is the case history of Maurie and Seymour Prager, a New Jersey couple who have been breeding and showing English Cocker Spaniels for longer than either cares to remember. They have bred, raised, and handled close to a hundred champions, but the only one of their On Time kennel dogs to go all the way to BIS had been sold as a pup to somebody else. The big victory gladdened the hearts of the Pragers and gave them immense satisfaction, but all of the glory went to the dog's owner. That's the way it goes in the dog game. It's nice to be the breeder of a great dog, but the owner gets most of the credit.

Seymour, an executive technologist in the food industry, is already established in the dog game's Hall of Fame as the coiner of a phrase that thousands of other fanciers claim to have coined. Many years ago, at a big indoor show, Seymour was watching a famous all-rounder at work in the Basset Hound ring. He and hundreds of other spectators groaned as the judge found his winners in some of the strangest-looking Bassets in the land. When the judge selected a dog who could hardly move as Best of Breed, unpleasant remarks filled the air. Seymour turned to a friend and said, "At least, the judge did not permit his great knowledge of the breed to influence his decisions." He said it in a loud tone, so as to be heard above the din, and among those who heard him was the judge. Well, the Pragers have shown their dogs under this same all-rounder about thirty times since that day, but they don't even have a fourth-place ribbon to prove it. Many feel that the judge should forgive and forget and be thankful for what will surely be his epitaph.

The Pragers were one-dog owners and living in Manhattan (1948) when they decided to give the dog game a try. The show they selected was convenient, but hardly ideal for a baptismal: Westminster. Nonetheless, the experience gave them a glow that's still burning. Seymour handled their puppy bitch to a win in the Puppy Class and to second best (Reserve) of all the class bitches present. He was comforted by the friendly smiles and hints of three other handlers in the ring: breed fancier John Trimble (now a judge), the late Mrs. M. Hartley Dodge (a legendary personality in the dog game), and Anne Rogers (now a judge, but for many years America's top professional handler). The pup's ribbons, plus the unexpected camaraderie from the greats, hooked the Pragers. They started breeding English Cockers, moved to the country, and became loyal citizens of the dog game.

Both handle, but Maurie is in charge of the training and care programs. She also picks the show hopefuls from each litter, and calls her methods of selection "a cold-blooded analysis of alertness and responsiveness." The analysis starts as soon as the pups have their eyes open, or long before they are weaned. Every time she shreds paper for the brood, she waves strands over the heads of the puppies and watches for the ones who respond. At other times, she'll make odd noises or employ a squeaky toy. Those that react stay in the running. She looks for the lively ones.

Maurie believes that the radio was invented to help raise puppies. Whenever young pups must be kept indoors, as during a blizzard or hurricane, she keeps the radio on and the pups become accustomed to all sorts of strange sounds. And every so often,

Seymour Prager stoops to correct the show stance of Ch. On Time Deborah, the dam of nine English Cocker Spaniel champions. *Stephen Klein*

she turns the volume on full blast, or as loud as she can stand it. The pup who can take that won't jump out of his skin at a dog show when the loudspeaker blares out ten feet above his head. The p.a. systems at shows often shatter the nervous systems of both dogs and handlers.

By the time the pups are seven weeks old, Maurie has her show hopefuls selected. They have passed the reaction tests. During the next two weeks, she studies the conformation of the chosen ones and makes her final educated guesses. These are the ones who will carry the On Time colors into the breed ring.

The ring training is not hurried, begins at three months, and it starts with the lead. Maurie ropes off a square hunk of terra firma to simulate a show ring, and that's where the pup does his gaiting. To keep the pup at her side and to prevent him from dashing ahead, she uses her free right hand to swing a willow branch in front of his face. He'll play with the branch at first, but it keeps him where he should be and obviates the need for a choke collar. Just a plain show lead suffices. Once the pup gaits pretty well without the branch, he is trained to stand in show position. Lessons are always brief, and Maurie keeps the training fun. She considers a wagging tail essential for a show prospect.

Pup or dog, the Pragers don't feed before leaving home for a show. They do not believe that a dog shows his best on a completely empty stomach, however, and feed a couple of small biscuits an hour or so before ring time. That means an early arrival at the show. They bait with either dried liver or malted milk tablets, and scoff at the idea that the biscuits take the edge off the baiting.

After a dog is through with his ring chores, he receives a light meal. While this is contrary to usual procedure, the Pragers have been feeding this way for a couple of decades and have never had a carsick dog on the ride home.

There's no way of estimating the number of married couples in the dog fancy, but the Pragers may be the only couple to radiate bliss on the drive to a dog show. "Listen, dogs are not insensitive clods," says Maurie. "In their hearts, your dogs live very close to you, and they can sense hostility, even if it's only vocal. So if he senses all is not well with you, he'll react in various ways, and his reactions are bound to affect him adversely in the ring." If the Pragers must argue on the day of a show, they do so early in the morning and out of earshot of their dogs. Once dogs, crates, and people have been loaded in the station wagon, all is tranquillity up front. "I damn near killed the lot of us on a curve one day," Seymour is fond of recalling. "Maurie didn't say anything at the time, but she sure gave me hell the next day."

At any dog show, one doesn't need a program to know when ring time is nearing for a particular breed. Dogs of the breed will be standing on crates or special grooming tables while their handlers go over them and apply the last-minute touches. Many handlers are pretty rough on their dogs, cussing them out or whacking them for not standing like statues. But not the Pragers. They continue their psychology of joy, coddling and petting and praising their beasts and keeping them in high spirits. When a Prager dog loses, he may be the happiest dog in the ring. But win or lose, the special attention from his humans continues. For him, the dog show is a joyous event.

Is all this special attention really necessary? Is this overdoing things or babying the dog too much? Are canines really sensitive, moody animals?

And then there are dog fanciers who resent any intrusion on their privacy as ring time approaches and they prepare their charges for the breed ring. Count Seymour among them.   *Stephen Klein*

The Pragers have been doing their thing for a long time, and they have no regrets, boxes of ribbons, and shelves crowded with trophies. And it is true that the canine body beautiful isn't always enough in the breed ring. Many a show dog is the very picture of his breed's standard in the physical sense, a sure winner—until he gets into the ring. There, if he's a Terrier without spark or an unmerry Beagle, or drags himself around the ring, he is not true to his breed's temperament. An honest judge will look to another for his winner, unless all the others are obvious bums.

If a dog is shy, stubborn, moody, or filled with fear, he will not show well in the ring, and the odds are against his success even if his conformation is excellent. It's a matter of personality, really, and his owner, not the dog, is the one who shapes it. Canine researchers are pretty much agreed that all pups are whelped as happy creatures, that they start using their brains at about eight weeks, and that their experiences from then to their eighth month will form their personalities for life. Those experiences can be controlled by a pup's owner, of course. So if the owner wants a happy dog, he'd better provide the pup with some happy times. For a human parallel, consider the woman who suffers claustrophobia because she was locked in a closet as a little girl.

So we don't sell the Pragers short. That doesn't mean, however, that only a happy dog can be well trained. Take a certain plumber and his dogs. We had an emergency, or a flooded basement, and he responded to our call for help. Upon arrival, he parked his Caddy in the drive, then strolled across the lawn to where we were teaching a couple of pups to go down on the verbal command.

"I happen to be a dog lover, too," he advised us, "but I never train a dog to go down that way. I just scowl, and the dog goes down."

We inquired as to how he trained a dog to respond to his scowl.

"Easy," he explained. "When I scowl and he doesn't go down, I beat the hell out of him. It doesn't take long for a dog to learn the trick."

Then he went into the basement and beat the hell out of our pump. We scowled, and found another plumber.

He was an Englishman, whose wife carded the shedded, silky undercoats of their Samoyeds and knitted sweaters and socks. The man and his wife were the only British-born dog lovers we've ever met who didn't think highly of that giant of dog shows known as Cruft's. "A bloody bit of noise" was their verdict.

An ocean and a vowel apart from Cruft's is Crafts, a big name in the American dog fancy. Many dog fanciers hold that Glenna and the late Robert Crafts of Ohio were the saviors of the Norwegian Elkhound in the New World. Certainly the breed was going nowhere in particular when the Crafts came along in the 1950's and embraced Norway's gift to dogdom. With elk, bear, and mountain lion pretty scarce in Ohio, the Crafts had to look elsewhere to find action for the breed, and they found it at dog shows. Right ·from the start, they handled their own dogs, and did an amazing amount of winning. Robert, an executive and counsel

Mr. Norwegian Elkhound. Head study of the great Tryg in his prime.

for one of the giant corporations, had a pet phrase for those who wondered why Crafdal dogs were never handled by a professional: "You wouldn't pay someone to play your golf for you!"

The Norwegian Elkhound now ranks around thirty-fifth in the popularity poll. It would be down around seventy-fifth, battling with such breeds as the Pointer, Bullmastiff, Bouvier des Flandres, and Norwich Terrier if it were not for the Crafts and one of their homebreds in particular. He is American and Canadian Ch. Trygvie Vikingsson, the first arrival in the very first litter of pups ever whelped (1955) at Crafdal. At a time when the Norwegian seldom placed in Group, the mighty Tryg harvested over a hundred Group placements, plus twenty-five firsts and three Bests in Show. As a winner, he set all sorts of records for the breed. Since his retirement from the show, he's been setting all sorts of records as a producer of champions. For a decade now, he's been among the first three of all breeds as a top sire (of champions), and the dogs doing the big winning today in the breed are his offspring, and so are many other top producers. Lord knows where the breed would be today if it weren't for Tryg.

In an average year, more than a score of Crafdal Elkhounds become champions, although Glenna has no desire to own all the top members of the breed and will sell her good prospects. The breed needs plenty of exercise, and a hopeful puppy buyer will go home without one if he can't prove he has property enclosed by a fence.

Group and Best in Show wins aside, Glenna must be rated as one of the top amateur handlers in the dog game. She has piloted over a hundred of her homebreds to their championships and is still going strong. Despite her record, she considers herself a pretty bum handler and gives all of the credit to her dogs. This makes her unique in the dog game. After he's finished his first champion, the average amateur considers himself the equal of most professionals. After the third, he knows he's superior to any professional, and gives serious consideration to becoming a judge.

A stranger watching Glenna in the ring for the first time might be inclined to agree with her self-estimation. She doesn't seem to be doing much of anything, yet the dog on the other end of the leash shows magnificently, and may be the only Elkhound in the ring with ears pricked and tail up and curled. Holding his ears and tail that way is against his breed's nature, so it's quite a trick to train an Elkhound to stand and gait that way, and be the very picture of strength and alertness all the time.

So maybe Glenna is right. Good or bad, she's not just a handler. She's a graduate student of the breed and a trainer-handler, and a great believer in the theory that all the work is done before one enters the ring with his dog.

"Start training for the breed ring as soon as you bring your puppy home" is her advice to novices. This means collar and lead, standing, baiting, and emphasis on accustoming the pup to the touch (handling) by other people. "But when you ask other people to handle your pup, instruct them not to reach for his head. Pups often have a natural shyness about strange hands reaching over their eyes. It's a fear of being struck." All other parts of the body should be touched or rubbed by strange hands, and by members of both sexes. In the case of a male pup, the parts include the testicles, since they will be examined by judges.

"Always maintain a fun attitude when training a dog" is another of her golden rules. A happy pup is a spirited one, and he carries his mood into the ring. In the case of the Elkhound, happiness also means ears and tail up.

Glenna stays close to a new hopeful at his first couple of shows. It's a strange world to the dog, and she feels her presence helps his confidence. At later shows, she leaves the dog alone for most of the half hour before the breed judging. When she returns to the dog, he's damn happy to see her and carries his bounce right into the ring. It's fun time again.

Along about the ninth or tenth month, when most fanciers start feeding their dogs once a day, Crafdal dogs continue to get fed

Glenna with one of her current stars, Ch. Crafdal Tryg N Thors Rogue, a great grandson of Tryg.

twice a day and are never cut down to just once. Glenna feels this makes life more interesting for the dogs, and the kennel dogs in particular, for it gives them more human contact. In her view, also, the two-a-day system is easier on a dog's digestive tract, and anyone who wants to argue with her will have to see her vet. He agrees.

The two-a-day gives her closer control of a dog's condition. For the dog packing too much weight, it's a simple matter to adjust just one meal. The same holds true for the dog who runs a bit thin.

Prior to any show, two meals are skipped. A dog headed for a Saturday show isn't fed on Friday afternoon or Saturday morning, and doesn't eat again until he returns home from the show. This minimizes travel and ring accidents, and keeps the dog more alert to baiting when he's being shown.

Not feeding on the day of the show prior to showing is a common practice of almost all handlers, amateur and pro. In our observation, the only deviates are some of the top professional handlers who force-feed an underweight dog a half hour or so before the dog is due in the ring. If all goes well, the full belly helps to cover the ribs. The risk is that the dog may regurgitate while in the ring and blow his chances. It can be argued that the out-of-condition dog should be left at home, but then the handler would not be able to collect his fifty-dollar fee. Business comes first.

"Never on Sunday" is the dietetic theme song of many professionals and some amateurs. The lyrics claim that it's healthy for a dog to practice abstinence at least one day a week, and Sunday is the day. So, at home or on the road, show dogs are not fed on Sunday. Since the handlers are on the road almost every Sunday, the song is a convenience for them and also cuts overhead. Why the amateurs sing the song is a mystery. All of them eat on Sunday. Perhaps the singing gives them that old-pro feeling.

Despite the fact that her breed can go a week without food and suffer no great harm, Glenna doesn't go for the Sunday business. Still, she feels it's a far lesser sin than force-feeding, a method that ruins a dog's dining joys and turns him into a child who must be spoon-fed.

Despite propaganda to the contrary, not every breed is "good with children." It's more a matter of inherited temperment: the end result of carefully blended bloodlines. This bare fact is illustrated by a Crafdal Norwegian Elkhound.

The First Lady of Elkhounds goes along with the theory that the handler's nervousness runs down the leash, and has somehow managed to take advantage of the popular supposition by remaining confident and at ease in the ring. The vibrations running down a leash of hers keep the dog calm and happy and with ears up. So as amateurs go, she's a very unusual woman. Her secret formula for avoiding jitters? "It may be a personality deficiency. In the beginning, I knew next to nothing about handling. I was successful, it was fun, and it never occurred to me that I was in a life-or-death sport. Handling is still fun. So maybe what I have isn't confidence. It's enjoyment, and that's the message the dog receives. If a dog thinks he's working, he gets stubborn or bored, and just won't show at his best." Oddly, she's a nervous wreck when whelping time nears and a bitch's labor begins.

High on her list of musts for training the young show prospect is exercise, and that means running. Walking and gaiting the pup is fine for the master, but only running gives the pup the muscle he needs to become a sound dog. Like most dog fanciers, Glenna is not a track star, so she uses the bike method. All this requires is a bicycle, the ability to ride it, a six-foot leash, and a quiet road. "Pedal just enough to keep the pup at a sustained run, not a gallop, and he covers plenty of ground in a short time. It's easier than one thinks to manage bike and pup at the same time. An interesting by-product is the opportunity to observe the pup's movement from a perspective impossible to achieve when gaiting him on foot."

For her size of breed, Glenna recommends the bike method for pups five months and older, and she finds it a fine way to keep adult show dogs in shape. Thanks to an inexpensive speedometer, she knows that she and her great Tryg chalked up four hundred miles during one three-month period of his show career.

Apartment dwellers and suburbanites with small yards, please note.

While professional handlers had been plying their trade for a long time prior to 1929, that was the year the A.K.C. brought a little more order into the dog game by licensing them. This put a number of con artists out of business but was no worry to the pros who really knew dogs and how to handle them. Unto this day, one person cannot handle another person's dog for payment unless he holds a professional handler's license.

The first batch of pros approved for A.K.C. licenses numbered twenty-six. Of those, only four were women, and of all twenty-six, only Isabella Hoopes remains active. She was and remains Number 9.

Mrs. Hoopes was pretty handy with animals, dogs and horses in particular, while still a girl. She attended her first dog show in 1901, caught the dog-game bug, and has been sort of overwhelmed by dogs ever since. She's in the record books as a breeder of about a dozen breeds and a successful handler of about forty. Beagles and Pointers were probably her favorite breeds, and today she pretty much limits her handling to Beagles. Otherwise, she's active as a successful painter, when time permits. There's not much time, for she's also a busy actress in television and on Broadway.

Isabella was going great guns as an actress before professional handling entered her mind. "In 1927, while walking back to the original Madison Square Garden with a well-known dog person,

Isabella Hoopes arriving at a 1925 outdoor show with a quintet of her famous Saddlerock Beagles. Those were the days of substantial entries from one kennel. Today, the one- and two-dog owners predominate at the shows. *Stanley Stady*

The day veteran dog fanciers thought the world was coming to an end—April 24, 1930. At the Lackawanna Kennel Club dog show in Scranton, Pa., a lady professional handler guided a dog to Best in Show. The woman who shattered male domination was Isabella Hoopes, shown here with the Pointer who helped her make dog-game history, Ch. Herewithem Do Do. *H. Baroff*

I was told there would be a banquet that night to honor a famous professional handler who was retiring with a million dollars." Two years later, when the family business failed and she was at liberty as an actress, she remembered that million dollars. By then, she was one of the top amateur handlers around, and also a popular judge. She resigned her judgeship, turned pro, and had no trouble finding clients. In the going, a little history was made: no other judge had ever turned pro.

The mistress of Saddlerock Kennels, a very famous name in the dog game during the two decades before World War II, still trains dogs for the breed ring as she did a half century ago:

"Start training as soon as the pup is old enough to stand strongly. I begin by standing him on a table and posing him with legs and tail and head in the perfect position for the breed. If you don't know the right position for the breed, read the standard and look at pictures of top winners. Do this training every day, morning and afternoon. A little reward is helpful.

Mrs. Hoopes with Ch. Black Fells Imperator, one of the winningest Pointers in history. The dog took Best of Breed at Westminster 1936 over another great Pointer, Ch. Nancolleth Marquis, and the win started a debate that still rages among old-timers. Marquis was owned by the late Mrs. M. Hartley Dodge, a mighty name in the dog game, and he had taken both breed and Sporting Group at Westminster 1935. The experts said he would repeat in 1936, and then go on to Best in Show. Judge Samuel Allen, the 1936 Pointer breed judge and a brave man, preferred Imperator. End of story: a Sealyham went BIS.

"At about three months, introduce the lead. Let the pup run free on the lead until he gets used to it and doesn't fight it. But during each lead lesson, call him close and pose him.

"After he's used to the lead, put it high, or just under the throat and in back of the ears. Hold the lead short and walk him with his head up, back and forth in a straight line, always on your left side and close. At the end of each trip, pose him in show position.

"Once the pup is accustomed to the trips on tight lead, hold the lead a little looser each day. But if he puts his head down, jerk it up. In the end, he should trot freely on a loose lead with head up."

True, and a whole new generation of professional handlers will agree. And that's the way every judge wants to see a dog move: trotting on a loose lead with head up. The trouble is that the new generation has introduced the short, tight lead. The dog does keep his head up, but because he must. Damn few judges demand the loose lead, and most amateurs now emulate the professionals.

"If you don't have the hands, your dog is at a disadvantage. It's hard to learn," says Mrs. Hoopes, who always did have the right hands for the job. Difficult dogs used to be her specialty, and some that other professionals found impossible to handle came to her and then started winning big. Having the right hands, of course, means having the right touch. It's akin to dowsing. Some people have it and some don't.

Fortunately, anyone born with the wrong hands can train them into right hands by patience, experience, and study. Years ago, we stood at ringside with Marjorie Renner, the late all-rounder, watching a professional handle a Golden Retriever in the Sporting Group. "Fifteen years ago, Luke was the worst handler in the world," she told us. "But look at him now. It's as if his hands are talking to the dog, and his words are running down the lead." Luke had acquired the touch, and on that day his Golden took BIS.

Owning the right hands helps, but sometimes more is needed for showing the difficult dog. One of Mrs. Hoopes secrets: "If the dog is very hard to hold or full of too much pep, a small meal or drink before ring time will often settle him down and make him easier to handle."

How should a handler treat a judge in the ring? "Don't!" is her advice. "Behave as you would in a courtroom: on trial. Your dog is on trial in the ring, and you are part of your dog.

"If the judge asks a question, answer politely and don't try to be smart or funny. Follow his directions, but don't try to push your dog under his nose. And keep your dog in a good position at all times. I don't mean that the dog has to be posed, but his faults should not be exposed.

"And no matter what a sap you think the judge is, don't show it! It's difficult, but if the judge knows the breed and is fearless in his opinion, your dog will get what he deserves on the day. I hope."

Number 9 contends that she has never been nervous in the ring as a professional or an amateur. "I was a professional actress, accustomed to spectators and critics." Like Mrs. Crafts, then, one of the few handlers who have never experienced a case of jitters in the ring. There aren't many, but three more who come to mind were a young Broadway actress, a striptease artist, and a lady wrestler—all accustomed to spectators. But none had the right hands.

Among the professionals, a gentleman with the right hands was Lloyd Case. Although he retired a few years ago, his imprint remains on the dog game, since about a dozen of today's top pro handlers served their apprenticeships under him. And all through his handling career, Lloyd was a leading breeder of Great Danes, Boston Terriers, Cocker Spaniels, Golden Retrievers, and Dachshunds. Today, many winning dogs in those breeds have a Celloyd dog or two in their family trees. Lloyd had a good thing going for him. He bred the best, sold them, and then handled them for their new owners. "If any pro had to win, I was the one" is the way he remembers thirty-five years of handling. "My reputation as a breeder was on the line." His reputation did not suffer.

To the sorrow of many wealthy dog fanciers, Lloyd didn't sell all of his top dogs. One still going strong at stud in his thirteenth year is Ch. Celloyd Daniel, one of the all-time Smooth Dachshund greats. In his brief show career, Danny picked up eight BIS wins and was top dog at many Dachshund Specialty shows. When Lloyd handled Danny in the ring, he was considered to be an amateur.

Lloyd sees no particular advantage in early ring training or exposure at the shows. Indeed, he feels owners should wait until dogs are about a year old before deciding on show careers for their loved ones. By then, if the owner has bothered to study the breed, the dog is well developed and his potential is apparent. Either he has it or he lacks it.

If the dog looks like a winner, his ring training begins. Lloyd suggests a fifteen-minute training session once a day, with the handler teaching both gait and proper show stance.

During his three decades as a professional, he worked the dogs

Ch. Celloyd Daniel, a vegetarian who proves that George Bernard Shaw was right. Now an oldster and long past his prime, Danny is still a power at stud. *Evelyn Shafer*

outdoors, and usually in an area confined by posts and rope, or a crude simulation of an actual breed ring. Sometimes a lawn umbrella, table, and chairs were placed along one side of the ring's interior, and the props helped complete the show picture for the dog. And for a closer touch of reality, Lloyd often has other handlers (his wife, kennel assistants, neighbors) in the ring with dogs.

"Kindness, patience, and firmness are the three essential qualities a successful handler must have, and the only tricky one is the firmness. The dog must know that you're the boss, so you must be firm. But that doesn't mean roughness, abusive tactics, or losing your temper. A tug on the lead and a verbal command should be enough to correct any dog."

It may sound like treason to his former profession, but Lloyd doesn't think there's any great art involved in handling, and that anyone can succeed in the breed ring, provided he has a good dog. "If you have the right dog, you'll win a good percentage of the time. Not always, but often enough to satisfy."

Throughout his professional career, Lloyd handled only the dogs that he considered to be good ones. "I told each client that we'd know whether I was right or wrong after three shows. If the dog didn't win or come close to winning, that was the end of his show career, as far as I was concerned." The only client who ever gave him an argument was the Duke of Windsor. "I told him that his Pug was impossible, but he insisted that he knew the breed and that he wanted me to show the dog. First time out, the dog won three points. 'Retire him,' said the Duke. 'Always quit when you're ahead.' "

That was the one time in his career when he showed a dog against his better judgment. "There are times when the best dog in the world shouldn't be shown. He's bound to become listless once in a while and not give a damn, like a great actor who just can't pull himself up for a given performance and just walks through his role. I'll say this for the Duke's Pug: he was full of fire that day."

The man who almost achieved the impossible dream smiles when he's reminded of a certain White Paper that circulated among members of the Professional Handlers Association a few years ago. A copy of it fell into our hands, and we were amazed to read such proclamations as "The professional handler is the mainstay and backbone of the sport of dogs" and "It is they [the professionals] who oil and keep the wheels of dogdom going on the right track."

It is Lloyd's opinion, and we agree, that such statements do not hold water. If, today, all the professionals were to disappear, tens of thousands of owners and their good dogs would come out of the woods tomorrow. Unfortunately, those tens of thousands now feel they don't stand a chance against the professionals. They are wrong.

The impossible dream? Winning Best in Show with the odds in your favor. No professional handler in history ever came closer than Lloyd, and it happened at a show some fifteen years ago. He handled five of his clients' dogs to firsts in their respective Groups. For the final judging, he had five of the six dogs in the ring, and only the Terrier Group winner was not his. Five out of six chances for BIS. The Terrier was handled by its owner. The Terrier won.

Lloyd Case with a brace of his homebred Celloyd Golden Retrievers.

If an owner decides he needs a professional handler for his dog, how does he find the right one? Lloyd suggests: (1) visiting a few shows, watching the pros who handle the breed, and selecting several who seem to be getting the most out of their dogs—even if the dogs aren't winners; (2) checking out those pros with veteran handlers of the breed and rating their choices; and (3) visiting at least a couple of the top choices at their kennels for discussions. A pro to avoid is one who solicits business, or who doesn't appeal as a human being, or who agrees to handle a dog without seeing the dog first, or who maintains a kennel that is not in immaculate condition, or who insists on a long-term contract. "My policy, if I liked the dog, was to handle him for three shows. By then, we'd have a pretty good idea of the dog's future at the shows. Not much sense in wasting my time or the client's money if the dog wasn't going anywhere."

Fair enough. For those interested in the services of a pro, the trick is to find another Lloyd Case.

CHAPTER VII

OPINIONS
FROM ON HIGH

Friendly, Helpful, and Blistering Advice for All Handlers from a Quartet of America's Leading Breed Judges: Bernard Ziessow, James Trullinger, Elsworth Howell, and Dan Gordon § What to Do and What Not to Do § How Handlers Irritate Judges § How to Avoid Trouble and other Pertinent Information

THERE ARE more potential authors in the dog fancy than in any other special-interest group on earth. The amateurs are sure that their lives in the dog game will make superb reading, the professionals feel that their names on grooming and clipping books will sell millions of copies, and the breed judges dream of authoring tomes of advice that will cure the sins of amateurs, professionals, and other judges. The net result of all this honest intent is damn few books. Almost all dog fanciers can spell, but they just don't have the time to put words down on paper. While his private life is of secondary interest to the average fancier, he must still lead one, and it and dogs occupy most of his wakeful hours.

The dream-book ratio is highest among the judges. We don't know all of them, of course, but we have been around the dog game long enough to know over a hundred well enough to criticize some of their ring decisions and to date we have not been assaulted. Eighty percent have vowed to write a book, but just under 1 percent have ever done so, and it's not likely that the others ever will. Since a giant industry—television—believes that a sampling can be projected, there's no reason why the dog game can't project that rough 1 percent to cover all breed judges. We are happy to do so right now.

It is true that most judges intend to write their books after retirement. Then they are in no danger of facing such criticism as "In your book you wrote that the loose lead is a must, yet your Pointers today were so strung up that their front feet didn't touch the ground." The only possible retort, and it seldom helps, is a withering "My dear lady, things look different from outside the ring!"

But few judges retire. Those that do are not physically up to the task of writing tens of thousands of words, or they want to forget the dog game. It is not that they no longer like dogs. They are tired of the people who own dogs.

Among the 20 percent of breed judges who have not announced a yen to write a book is the man whose advice leads off this chapter. This is a coincidence. As is the custom, the panel of judges is presented in reverse alphabetical order.

Bernard W. Ziessow of Michigan, finance executive for one of the large motor companies whose product may be in your future, is licensed to judge all Sporting breeds and Group 1, and thus qualifies to judge Best in Show. Berney, as he is known to his family, friends, other judges, and finance officers, may be the only judge around to admit to a peculiar sort of kennel blindness. If the man doesn't know all there is about the Labrador breed, then it's his fault, for the Lab kennel of Franklin is his wife's avocation. That's where the great Dark Star was whelped, as well as such other famous champions as Sunset Road, Discovery, Troublemaker, and Golden Chance.

Let it be known that Berney's kennel blindness was in reverse order and did not concern a Labrador. He went astray on an English Springer Spaniel, acquired as a pet for his daughter. The Springer pup lived in the house, slept in the girl's room, and developed into a perfect pet and companion. He answered to the name of Snoopy.

Several years after the pup's arrival, Berney judged a huge entry

Bernard Ziessow

of Springers at an Ohio show. When he returned home, his wife Madge inquired about the quality of the entry. "Hell," he replied, "Snoopy could have beaten the lot of them." The Ziessows looked at each other, then took some long looks at Snoopy. They'd grown so accustomed to the dog that they'd overlooked his qualities. A few months later, Snoopy was Ch. Salilyn's Santa Claus and the envy of the Springer Spaniel set.

Any breed judge who confesses to a personal oversight must be considered a candid man. Herewith, some candidness straight from the pages of Judge Ziessow's private diary and meant for both amateur and professional handlers:

On grooming and conditioning: "While it may be possible for a judge to discover a 'diamond in the rough,' it's easier for him to see a polished stone, and every successful handler takes advantage of this adage."

He is weary of seeing overweight and underweight dogs in the ring. If they are not in condition, home is the place for them. The fat or emaciated dog cannot possibly show to his own advantage. But if in shape, his grooming must be right. Catching the judge's eye is one of the unwritten rules of the game.

"I was sitting beside one of my favorite judges, an all-rounder, at a large midwestern show. We were watching the Sporting Group. All the dogs had been set up, and from our vantage point they looked like a fine collection of Royal Dalton figurines. The judge in the ring studied them all for several minutes, then asked one handler to move his dog again. At this point, the all-rounder turned to me and said, 'That dog is bad in front and worse behind, but, my God, isn't he turned out beautifully?' " Guess who won?

On helping the judge in the ring: "I was judging an Open class. Two handlers were engaged in pointing out the faults of each other's dogs. One pointed to poor shoulders, the other to straight hind legs. Any judge considers this volunteer help as an insult to his intelligence. It doesn't do any good and often has an adverse effect.

"Newcomers and many children are inclined to overshow. They are constantly fussing with their dogs, hoping to draw the judge's attention to the dog's good points. Instead, all the fussing tends to distract the judge's attention from the dog. Now I don't want to discourage children. They should be encouraged, but they should remember that the judge is there to see the dogs and not clever, juvenile antics. When a dog is set up right, leave him alone."

On movement: "With few exceptions, the dog should be gaited on a loose lead at his natural, uniform trot. Neither too fast so that he's out of control, nor so slow that he waddles. Only constant practice will determine the best gait for the dog. His head should be erect, his tail happy, and he should look like he's enjoying life. The handler should always adjust his gait to the dog's. Unfortunately, too many dogs are asked to adjust their gait to their handlers'. Practice and more practice determines the optimum gait. Whether the handler walks or jogs, his speed must match the dog's speed."

While nobody ever argues out loud with that wisdom, it's apparent to the judge that many handlers disagree. He has various categories for the dissenters:

The Track Star. This handler frequently wears tennis shoes and is out to prove that he can run faster than his dog. Advance cases run on the tips of their toes, as in ballet, and some approach the gazelle in style.

The Giant Stepper. A tall handler, usually over six feet, and a walker. To keep up with his dog, he lengthens his stride, and looks for all the world like the Jolly Green Giant. Advance cases lean over and point out the right direction to their dogs, then do a little shuffle before stepping out. Once in a while, one will trip over his confused dog.

The Baby Trotter. Usually a woman handling one of the smaller breeds. Rather than walk, she prefers to trot, and her steps measure about ten inches. On rough ground, this can be dangerous for both handler and dog.

The Whoa Nellie. A handler who is shown by his dog. Usually, the dog is one of the big, strong breeds, and he drags the handler around the ring. Almost always, the handler has waited until the very day of the show before putting a lead on his dog.

The Pacer. The handler who permits his dog to pace. Nobody has told him that the trot is a dog's natural gait, but that some dogs will pace on lead. If he knows it, he fails to watch his dog and must be corrected. Time consuming and unnecessary.

Judge Ziessow on presenting the dog for inspection: "While the judge learns from watching the dog's gait, he must physically examine the animal in order to pass final judgment, and this is of particular importance with the longer-haired breeds. The successful handler keeps his dog alert and under control at all times. He doesn't let the dog fall apart at one end while the judge is looking at the other. Always, he keeps one eye on the judge, learns his routine, anticipates his movements, thus assisting the judge and helping his dog's chances.

"Practice, practice, practice. The show dog who stands like a statue is not a freak of nature. Hours and hours have been spent working with this dog until he has learned what is expected of him. And the constant winning amateur isn't a freak of nature, either. He's spent hours watching his betters in the ring, studying their techniques, becoming intimate with his breed standard, and learning how proper handling can minimize his dog's faults.

"Frequently, show dogs display shyness in the ring, and that doesn't help their chances. The shyness may be hereditary, but more often it's the result of being in a strange environment. One can hardly expect a show dog to move from a cloistered existence at home into the noisy world of a dog show without displaying some anxiety. Strange sounds, scents, dogs, and stranger people are sometimes too much for him. And it's also understandable why some dogs shy away from the judge, a complete stranger, who wants to examine him.

"While the above conditions can sometimes be corrected through more show experience, the easy way is to start at home. Walks down busy streets and through shopping centers (on lead), examinations on the home grounds by friends, and lots of handling all help."

On covering faults: "Wise handling will minimize a dog's faults. However, this requires finesse, for an obvious attempt to cover up will point out a fault to the judge. One of my veteran confreres is always purposely slow in starting a class. This gives exhibitors ample time to set up their dogs, and also gives him the opportunity to observe any attempts to cover up a dog's faults. When the action starts, the judge already knows just which dogs are out at the elbows, swaybacked, or cow-hocked."

On impressing the judge: "Judges were not born yesterday, but some handlers find that hard to believe. Nonbelievers, hoping to influence the judge's decision, inform him that their dogs are good ones. The ploy has several variations, 'My dog got a Group first under Judge So-and-So at Sceptic City last week' being the commonest. Then there is the name dropping, as in the case of Fido Frito, a dog with a winning reputation and numerous press clippings. To make sure the judge knows that the dog is indeed the great Fido Frito, the handler keeps dropping the name, as in 'Show your stuff, Fido Frito' or 'Head up, Fido Frito.'

"The name dropping can backfire. I can recall one occasion when a Fido Frito handler so irritated a second handler, whose dog was of the same size and marking, that the latter started calling his dog Fido Frito. The offender got the message, reddened, and ceased.

"Another variation of the theme is a bit more elaborate. It calls for planting somebody outside the ring, but conveniently close to the judge's table. Whenever the judge is within earshot, the loud-voiced plant extolls the virtues of a particular dog, always emphasizing the dog's number. Thus: '*Seventeen* is the only sound mover in there,' or 'Trullinger gave *seventeen* the breed at Philadelphia,' or 'She turned down an offer of ten thousand for *seventeen*!'

"The judge whose assignment calls for him to look at the same breed winner in Group later in the day can almost count on a few reminder words from the breed winner's handler or friends: 'Number *twelve*, the Boxer you just put up, is Champion Beeflat. He has Bangaway behind him.'

"In my experience, this type of promotion is useless. If one has a good dog, it won't take long for everyone to know it. All the public relations in the world won't improve a poor dog. The secret to success is a good dog properly presented. He may not win all the time, but it will take a better dog to beat him."

Berney wasn't present at a certain outdoor show a few years back, or he might have included an anecdote about a great dog whose fame was so widespread that it helped another dog score a tremendous victory. But we were there, witnessed the event, helped the winning handler recover from his shock, and feel, since the judge is no longer around to read these words, that some of the story can now be told.

The show was a big one, and the late and famous judge's name drew a huge entry of dogs in a certain breed—close to a hundred dogs, about forty of them champions. The judge was not a young man, the day was hot, and it took a long time for him to run through the classes and get down to his selection of Best of Breed. America's top dogs of the breed awaited his examination, and we assumed it would take him an hour or so to make up his mind. So we strolled off to a tent, looking for shade and the pause that refreshes, and intending a return to ringside in forty minutes or so.

Ten minutes later, a mighty shout arose from the ringside, and the hundreds of spectators dispersed. The judging was over. Along came one of the handlers with his dog, a young champion named Bozo. We asked what dog had taken Best of Breed.

"I need a cold beer. Help me recover. Believe it or not, Bozo won!"

Well, it was hard to believe. There was nothing wrong with Bozo, but there had been at least twenty better dogs in the ring with him, and he wasn't much compared to his own sire, the very great Homer, who was loafing at home in an air-conditioned kennel. Homer had dominated the breed for about five years, but now he was old and shown only sparingly, and never during hot weather.

"The damndest thing happened," said the handler, after he'd drained his can of beer. "As the judge handed me the rosette, he said, 'I've waited four years to judge this dog, and he's even better than I thought he would be.' So I took the rosette and ran."

A case of identification and association. The judge had identified the handler, assumed that Homer was on the other end of the lead, and thought that he was confirming the opinions of many other authorities.

It was Bozo's finest hour. He hasn't been heard from since. His handler is still around, still winning big with other dogs, and still cautioning us to keep the true story under wraps. We wouldn't think of breaking his confidence. We like him and we've always liked Homer. Come to think of it, we liked the judge.

We like many judges, both as people and breed authorities. And that's a strange thing, for some of them have never liked our dogs. On our approved list are the judges who appear on these pages. A costly confession, for it means we will never be able to show our dogs under them again. The dog game, for all its joys, is also a major industry. The compensating factor is that from here on we'll be able to tell them precisely what we think of their judging.

So hail and farewell to James W. Trullinger, the all-rounder of international fame. He has officiated at all the major shows in the fifty states, plus Canada, Puerto Rico, Colombia, Brazil, Uruguay, Cuba, and other lands where dogs enjoy popularity between revolutions. So far as we know, he is the only American judge to appear in several works of fiction (ours), and we are sure that, when he was younger, he was the youngest all-rounder in history. Indeed, the A.K.C. licensed Jim as a judge during his freshman year in college. He was already a breeder of Dachshunds and Gordon Setters, and was destined to become involved with Miniature Pinschers, Pointers, Pekingese, English Springer Spaniels, Standard Poodles, and Pugs. His mighty Pug, Ch. Diamond Jim, was regarded as the best around since 1883, the year the first breed standard was drawn.

For the past couple of decades, Jim has been busy mixing duties as a public-relations executive with flying around the world to dog shows. So busy that he's become sparse with words and makes every one count, and we aren't sure if the following constitutes advice or pleas or a blend of both:

"To exhibitors [amateurs] and handlers [professionals]: I wish to the Lord that all persons would show their charge naturally— with ease, with proper restraint, and in a relaxed manner.

"I can do without overshowing: the use of hands to stretch necks and heads, hands running down the topline or thumping it, and hands grabbing the ears in all sorts of manners. I am there to judge the dog and I don't need a lesson from the eager beavers!

"On winning the Open class, too many people let it be immediately known that now their dog is 'finished.' Well, maybe. As gently as possible, I tell them, 'You haven't won the purple yet.'

"The worst offender may be the handler who just will not follow ring procedure as outlined by the judge. He moves his dog as he pleases, always to his dog's disadvantage."

J. W. Trullinger belongs to that 1 percent of all breed judges who will someday write a book. His will be about the Pug breed, and the publisher will probably be another judge, Elsworth Howell.

Judge Howell, a top executive in the publishing world (Grolier), is a veteran breeder and exhibitor of English Setters, Cocker Spaniels, Dachshunds, West Highland White Terriers, Schipperkes and Basset Hounds. He's licensed to judge Group 1, plus several of the Hound breeds and the Schipperke. The end is not in sight.

Everybody suspects that his real love is the English Setter, and among his champions have been two outstanding stalwarts of the

James W. Trullinger

breed, Rock Falls Racket and Stan the Man of Valley Run. Considering his vocation and avocation, it seems only natural that he is the only American dog fancier to own a publishing house, and that the house bearing his name publishes only nonfiction dog books. His firm, founded some ten years ago, has developed into the most important one in the dog game.

In his judgment, dog shows draw more rank amateurs and beginners than any other sport or competition enjoyed by man. He finds this rather strange, for no one in his right mind would enter any other form of competition, such as a tennis or golf tournament, without some measure of skill in the sport. "Apparently, some owners expect their dogs to show themselves, which is comparable to racing a horse without a jockey."

Stranger still, some amateurs stay with the sport long enough to achieve veteran status, but never seem to acquire any expertise in the proper handling of dogs. Just why this should be is a puzzle to Judge Howell. "The art of showing dogs demands less mental strain, practice, and dexterity than almost any other participant sport. The rules of the dog game are so simple that children can follow them with ease, as Junior Showmanship classes prove. True, a few gifted people seem to know instinctively just how to handle dogs, but almost anyone sound in mind and body can learn the techniques adequately to show a dog without personal embarrassment and without danger of irritating the judge."

A pause for applause. Once upon a time there was a team of famous professional handlers, and they spoke here and there on the art of handling. They likened it to the blending of dance and

Judge Elsworth Howell demonstrates proper handler-technique with his top-winning English Setter, Ch. Stan the Man of Valley Run.   *William P. Gilbert*

music, to the marriage of horns in a symphony, and to the poet plotting his delicate meter.

We heard them once, and went home feeling empty. It seemed high time to shoot our dogs and get the hell out of the dog game. Even limited success seemed impossible to achieve. But the very next day, our stumbling, eleven-year-old offspring went to a show and put a four-point major on her dog. We weren't there, but we were told later that she had handled her dog in the ring just like a ballerina-conductor-poet.

Elsworth Howell has some easy steps for beginners and veterans who still handle as if they were beginners:

1.) Go to a dog show. Watch the accomplished amateurs and professionals. Study their techniques of setting up (posing) and gaiting dogs.
2.) Acquire some literature on the subject. Study it.
3.) Train your dog to stand quietly; alone at first, later with other people and their dogs. Have a stranger to your dog go over him by hand, from head to foot.
4.) Gait the dog on a loose lead, first in a counterclockwise circle, then forward and back in a straight line.
5.) Repeat exercises daily until you and your dog have them down pat. Then enter a show.

Now the show date approaches, but there's more to do than sit and dream:

1.) Practice the show routine a few minutes every day. Only the dog who is a seasoned campaigner, shown every weekend, can dispense with the preshow rehearsals.

2.) Groom the dog (trim or clip if the breed requires) long enough before the show so that his coat will be in prime condition. Don't hack at your dog the night before a show. "I found I couldn't give a ribbon to a fine Irish Setter whose neck and throat had obviously been clipped a few days before the show. The color there was several shades lighter than the desired rich mahogany red specified in the breed's standard."

3.) Clean the dog the day before the show. "Nothing disgusts a judge more than dirty dogs, but an appalling number are found in breed rings." Black and brown coats do not hide dirt. A judge's hands after examination tells the story.

It's show day, and handler and dog have arrived at the show. There's plenty of time before the dog's breed is called into the ring, and usually the novice wastes it. In Judge Howell's opinion, this is a grievous error:

"Watch the judge of your breed (as he judges another breed) to predetermine his judging techniques: his pattern for gaiting dogs, his preferred area for standing examination, and the methods he uses for examination. Judges have their pet, consistent ways.

"When a judge considers a decision close, for example, he may ask for two dogs to be gaited side by side between two handlers. A preview of the given judge's technique might not reveal this, and the only way to prepare for it is to accustom your dog to gaiting with another dog at home. Dogs like to play, and some will fight, and chaos can result if side-by-side gaiting is new to them. Control by the handler is mandatory.

"From a preview, the handler will know what's expected of him and his dog when he enters the ring. With ever-larger entries, judges are under tighter schedules. The more time they spend instructing handlers, the less time they have for considering the dogs. The resultant irritation can tax their cool."

Ring time is approaching:

"Exercise and groom your dog. A call of nature in the ring is annoying to the judge, embarrassing to the handler, not appreciated by spectators, and time wasting for all concerned.

"Finally, be ready at ringside for your class, with armband firmly attached and the number in plain view for the judge and steward."

Now, at last, the big moment is at hand. The dogs are called into the ring, and brave men falter, and it's time here for Howell's Inside Tips:

1.) Enter the ring with style and confidence. It *is* a show, so make a grand entrance. (Finest grand entrance we ever witnessed was that of a beautiful woman and her beautifully groomed Saluki. She radiated confidence, and the dog looked ready to conquer the world. His end of the lead was looped around his neck in the loose, English manner. They stood well off from the ring, and the lady waited so that they would be the last to enter. Finally, with her head high and steps sure, she marched forward and into the ring. But the loose lead had slipped over the Saluki's head, and he remained where he was. Moral: be sure you have your dog with you.)

2.) Always keep one eye on the judge, but don't try to mesmerize him. "I recall one attractive lady exhibitor who always fixed both of her big, brown eyes on the judge, but was oblivious to her dog's actions. She never won a point or a judge."

3.) The handler's eyes and hands are of equal importance. The alert handler has a constantly shifting look: to his dog, to insure correct stance and gait; to the judge, to divine his wishes and intentions; and to his fellow handlers and their dogs, in the hope of finding an advantage.

4.) The dog is always kept between the handler and the judge. The most omniscient of judges is never clairvoyant.

5.) Gait the dog on a loose lead. Most judges prefer it. "In my experience, dogs deficient in gait usually move better on a loose lead anyway."

6.) If you can't smile in defeat, at least put on a poker face. This is the Occident, but the poor sport still loses face with the judge.

And a Howell reminder that will come as news to tens of thousands of unaware dog fanciers, though it is nonetheless a fact of life in the dog game: "Never argue with a judge. Under American Kennel Club sanction, he is the supreme authority in the ring. Never cast aspersions in or out of the ring against the judge, another exhibitor, or his dog. Such actions may subject you to a complaint before the Show Committee and the loss of your privileges with the American Kennel Club."

To the regret of many a dog fancier, novice and veteran alike, the loss of A.K.C. privileges happens all the time. Of course, this is a two-way street, and the judge who slugs a handler, staggers around the ring, or flirts with an unappreciative handler is also subject to penalty—losing his license to judge, for example. Still, when one considers the vagaries of human nature, the great wonder of the dog game is that there has never been a shooting at a dog show.

Every breed judge who ever lived, of course, has been a mental target many times. So many dogs must always lose, and so many of their owners take the defeats personally and blame the judge, and some of those owners are violent people.

Still, almost every judge feels that his most trying moments come outside the ring and after his work is done for the day. Perhaps he is heading for his paycheck, his lunch, or his escape car. Whatever his goal, he is sure to be stopped by at least one disappointed owner and asked, "What didn't you like about my dog?"

Nine times out of ten, the judge doesn't remember the owner or the dog. If he has looked at 150 dogs in several breeds over the last few hours, his lack of instant total recall is understandable. But the owner will never understand. So the judge, not looking for trouble, must say something, and usually it is something harmless, such as "In my opinion, your dog lacked a touch of spirit. I do hope you'll enter him under me again. Excuse me, I have a long-distance call to answer."

But what if he remembers the dog, and considers it a dreadful beast? Should he be honest, break the owner's heart, and risk assault? Usually his reply is honest, consoling, and safe: "Today, he was not the best dog in the ring. Tomorrow, he may be. Excuse me, the president of the American Kennel Club has asked to see me."

Most newcomers to the dog game believe that they are entitled to a judge's private analysis of their dogs. They have, after all, paid an entry fee, and they want payment on their dollars. But there is nothing in the rules and regulations to substantiate the belief. They are paying to have their dogs judged. They are not paying for a personal critique.

However, a few brave judges will tell an owner what's wrong with his dog, and let the chips fall where they may. But in all fairness to the judges, owners who ask for such opinions should be willing to accept them without rancor. And any owner should have his dog along with him when he pops the delicate question. Then the judge will know what dog he is supposed to be criticizing. This is a big help.

One of the bravest judges is Dan M. Gordon, M.D., F.A.C.S. He is a veteran breeder and exhibitor of Boxers, the author of *The Boxer Book* (regarded as the breed's Bible), and the first American ever to judge the breed on the continent of Europe. Dan judges only the Boxer, and in the halls of medical science, a world apart from the dog game, he is ranked as one of this country's top ophthalmologists.

He does not garnish the truth when asked for his private criticism of a given dog, nor does he mince words when asked for his opinion on any other facet of the dog game. Implausible as it may seem to anyone familiar with the sensitivities of dog fanciers, Dr. Dan's frankness has increased his popularity as a judge and as an

Dan Gordon

after-dinner speaker. It took us about three years to book him for a twenty-minute talk at the Dog Fanciers Club. Unfortunately (from a dog lover's point of view), his vocation leaves him little time for his avocation.

Dan Gordon on amateur handlers: "Half of them don't know their breed standard. I assume all of them have read it, and hope more of them will someday understand it. The same goes for more than a few professionals.

"If the handler knows the basic essentials of his breed, it follows that he has a good concept of the ideal dog when in motion and when frozen in statuelike posture. In the ring, it is his function to render his dog as nearly like that ideal as is handerly possible. To that end, he should efface himself as much as possible, so that the judge will be impressed by the dog's anatomical correctness, as indicated by beauty of gait and naturalness of posture.

"The average handler overhandles. He swarms all over his dog, and the judge wonders what features are being intentionally covered up. And he constantly looks at the judge in a pleading manner that borders on the nauseating, while neglecting his dog, of course, and sort of exhibting himself.

"The good handler? He's never between the dog and the judge, and he makes it appear that the dog is almost exhibiting himself. The best of the good handlers are the ones whose dogs are the most noticed by the judge.

"Many a handler succeeds in preventing his dog from exhibiting his best qualities. A judge who remembers that he's present to judge dogs will often try to help an inept handler. Well, if the judge is a stranger in the area and doesn't know the handlers, the inept handler sometimes turns out to be a professional. This can be embarrassing, and the pro hates the judge, even if his dog wins.

"I'm aware that some judges are allergic to kids in the ring, but I've noticed that young people do a good job of handling. This may be because they have fewer inhibitions and have been able to imitate the top handlers they've seen.

"But this can work in reverse. We still have some areas in this country where professionals are not found in abundance, and one sort of dominates the field. His handling technique will be copied by others. If it's all wrong, the judge is in for a difficult time finding his best dogs."

Judge Gordon's views on the dog's chances of making his championship: "It's axiomatic that many mediocre dogs do finish. However, a really good dog will always finish, if given a chance. He may take some unfair beatings, but he will get his just desserts, too.

"Many owners continue to enter one dog in two classes. They do so in the belief that they are giving the dog two chances to enter the Best of Winners competition. This is foolish thinking and a waste of money. To stay in the running, the dog must win both classes. If he loses in just one class, he's disqualified.

"I may be accused of heresy for revealing this, but some specialty [one-breed] judges really don't know their breed and depend upon the professionals to show them the best dogs. They [the judges] are often people of means, own large kennels, and have solid reputations as breeders of good dogs. However, their kennel managers are the ones who know the breed, and they should be doing the judging.

"A smart owner who is intent on winning, then, must know when to handle his dog and when to hire a professional. It's a matter of knowing about judges."

The proof of that pudding, if proof is needed, is wealthy

fancier Max Malt, although that's not his real name. Over the past ten years, he's owned some great dogs in several breeds. Max loves to handle himself, but his business takes him all over the world, and he often hires professionals to handle his dogs. You might say that he considers that weekend lost when his dogs aren't competing at the shows.

We've watched Max in action many times, and consider him one of the finest amateur handlers around. But when he's handling, his champion dog doesn't get much of a look and seldom takes the breed. Quite often, the same judge will have given the same dog a Group win or a BIS at another show the week before. But at that show a pro, not Max, handled the dog. Obviously, Max is a fine fellow but he doesn't know his judges. And his pro isn't about to enlighten him. Some judges do work overtime earning the reputation of being a handler's judge. It's a big beef in the dog game.

Another big beef is that many of the judges who remain active as breeders have a tendency to favor the progeny of their own dogs. While Dan Gordon won't go out on that limb, he does confess that he has seen the big beef in action: "I once watched the owner of a 'great' male judging at a big show. It became obvious that he was consistently looking for something. He was looking for the progeny of his male. Virtually every winner was sired by his dog, but they weren't the best progeny at the show. The winners were fairly good dogs, but all had inherited their sire's recognizable, inherited faults. Many studs pass the same good qualities that may be considered as standard. Some studs pass certain identifiable poor qualities, or faults, and that's how their progeny are recognized."

Long active in the dog game and recognized as one of the fancy's thinking men, Dan has reached the conclusion that it is the world's only activity where ignorance pays off. "In all other pursuits, the achievement of knowledge is important for success. But consider the average successful breeder or owner. His lack of basic knowledge about his breed is incredible. Yet it's so easy to acquire the knowledge: the breed standard, books, and photographs. Anyone with a desire to learn will acquire more breed knowledge in a year than the average ten-year veteran.

"Of course, one can study the breed standard and look at good photographs of the breed's top dogs until he's blue in the face and still have no more than a one-dimensional understanding. The finishing touch is to observe good dogs in action, and the place to see them is at the dog shows. The bigger the show, the more dogs, but the danger is that the learner will assume that the judge's winners are the best representatives of the breed present in the ring. Unfortunately, the big shows often have the worst judges; too often true of Westminster itself. However, all the champions present will have been approved by several judges, and the majority will be close to the breed's ideal conformation.

"For the new breeder, the big show is also a fine place to find the right stud dog. The progeny of some of the champion dogs present will be found in the classes, and the breeder can see what these males can do with different bitches."

The noted Boxer authority has found that the dog game is unique in at least one other respect: it often brings out the worst in people. "Through malice, jealousy, stupidity, or all three, the average fancier goes out of his way to give a bum steer to another fancier. In my vocation, we sacrifice thousands of dollars annually in consultation fees by helping colleagues over the phone. We never knowingly give another ophthalmologist bad advice when he asks for help. It's the same in most other fields, but not in the dog game."

Those are strong words, and they do not apply to the various canine authorities whose words of wisdom appear in the pages of this tome. Nor do his words apply to us, for we are frequently on the phone trying to help new breeders who request our advice. Almost every time, the novices end up giving us their unsolicited advice. In the dog game, everybody is an expert.

"The instant expertise also covers judging," says Dan. "I recall the time Harry Hill brought out a new and beautiful bitch under me. Putting her up over all the others was my easiest chore of the day. The spectators applauded my decision, but later Will

Judy told me this story: Will had been at ringside, and the man sitting in front of him had jumped to his feet and shouted, 'That does it! Even Aunt Alice here agrees that was a lousy job of judging, and this is the first dog show she's ever seen!' " An unbiased woman.

Insofar as we know, Dan is the only American judge to make copious notes on every dog who comes under him. And he may be the only one to advise the handlers of the first four dogs in each class as to his likes and dislikes of each dog. In a class of four, it may hurt when Dan hands over the white ribbon (fourth place) and says, "Save your money. Your dog has too many faults to enumerate in the short time allotted me." The wise amateur retires the dog or turns to Obedience. The professional does not always pass along the advice to his client and never shows that dog under Dan again.

In spirit anyway, Judge Gordon comes the closest to his British counterparts, who publish their opinions of dog's they've judged in the leading canine weeklies. They do write some damaging opinions from time to time, but writing about a dog is much safer than a personal conversation with a dog's owner, so assault and battery is less likely in England. In years gone by, canine weeklies carrying judges' critiques were published in this country, but none lasted very long. American dog fanciers prefer to read only nice things about their dogs and satisfy their ids by buying space in the monthly dog journals. They write their own copy, of course.

Here, in England, and everywhere else in the world where dog shows are held, the hallmark of a true dog fancier is his willingness to criticize judges, particularly those his dogs have lost under. So every judge who breathes, no matter the righteousness of his decisions, is constantly belittled, cursed, and second-guessed.

One just doesn't ask a judge how he feels about the ever-present criticism of his talents. It's too personal a thing. But one fine day, when we were discussing the weather with the late all-rounder Edwin Pickhardt, he surprised us by volunteering his feelings: "When they stop arguing about my decisions, I'll know I'm not a good judge.'

But he was an unusual man. In over a half century of judging, he went out of his way thousands of times to encourage owners of losing but promising dogs. "Now don't go home and shoot yourself," he'd say. "This dog of yours is a little young. Six months from now, when he's fully developed, he'll do his share of winning." And almost always, Judge Pickhardt* was right. He figured a judge should also be a 'discoverer.'"

The only other all-rounder we've ever known to go out of his way in offering hope is Louis Murr. Years ago, one of us handled a glorious bitch under him. She did not win and did not even place in her class. "A great bitch," commented Louis. "All she needs is a handler."

On that day, the head of the house retired from handling. The distaff side took over, and the bitch was a champion after three more shows. Duchess was her name, and she was always grateful for the switch in handlers. She proved this years later, as we were rushing her to the vet's in the black of night. She had been in labor for many hours, and we feared that something was wrong. During the journey, Duchess jumped onto the lap of the head of the house and whelped her entire litter, or one pup.

It was our contribution to dog history and the improvement of the breed. Has any other man ever had a pup born on his lap? And how does one explain the stain to a dry cleaner?

---

* Over the past fifty years, one of the dog game's choicest hunks of gossip has been about the strong enmity that existed between Collie lovers Albert Payson Terhune and Judge Pickhardt. Utter nonsense. They were the best of friends. Indeed, Terhune followed the judge's recommendations when purchasing his foundation stock for Sunnybank.

CHAPTER VIII

IN PRAISE OF OBEDIENCE

The sport for intelligent dogs and patient owners § *Haven for the amateur* § *More breeds are eligible* § *Breed ring misfits qualify* § *where to find instruction* § *obedience degrees and how they are won* § *commands and how to teach them* § *Hand signals* § *Training truisms for any dog* § *domestic commands*

THE SPORT of Obedience is recognized as a test of an individual dog's intelligence, and the proving grounds are the Obedience trials. It is also a test of human intelligence, for complete rapport between handler and dog is essential. Success here makes success in the breed ring look like a picnic, and the end result is worth all the effort: an exceptionally well-trained dog.

There are almost as many trials as there are dog shows. They are not found at some shows, because space won't permit. The gap is closed by the Obedience-training clubs that hold separate, licensed trials. The sport is booming, and it won't be many years before there are more trials than breed shows. Along the way, it will help the growth of point shows, and the proof of that is already in hand: several of the all-breed kennel clubs have broken with tradition and are now sponsoring two shows a year

—one indoors, where space doesn't permit Obedience, and one outdoors, where space does.

Obedience is the new side of the American dog game, in that it didn't receive the official blessing of the A.K.C. until 1936. The fact that it is around at all must be credited to Mrs. Whitehouse Walker, the sport's pioneer enthusiast in this country. In the thirties, she was one of this country's leading breeders of Poodles (Carillon). So she wasn't unknown to the dog fancy when she visited England, where Obedience was known, practiced, and appreciated. There she observed the sport in action and determined to bring it to these shores. So, smack in the middle of the Depression, she returned home and started whipping up excitement. It was not an auspicious time to launch anything new, but here was an activity for the average one-dog owner who could derive "a maximum of pleasure [from his dog] at a minimum of expense."

Under Mrs. Walker's guidance, the Obedience Test Club of New York staged two trials in 1934. They were exhibitions, really, and meaningless as far as winning degrees went, but they lit a fire under the dog fancy. Six trials were held in 1935, and seventeen (including one in Hawaii) in 1936. Then came the official blessing—rules and regulations of the A.K.C. Obedience was on its way, and it's been spreading like wildfire ever since. It started with one woman's determination, a band of loyal followers, and a few intelligent dogs. The campaign to win A.K.C. recognition was remarkable in its brevity: less than three years.

Outside of the fact that Obedience accomplishes something (a really trained dog), much of the sport's popularity rests in the rules. Compared to the breed ring, more breeds are eligible. A dog must be a purebred, but he can belong to any one of the recognized breeds or the Miscellaneous breeds. So 126 breeds are eligible. And most dogs ruled out for the breed ring are fine and dandy for Obedience. The spayed bitch, the altered male, the monorchid and cryptorchid, and the dog not up to his breed standard (the white German Shepherd, the Boxer with natural ears and tail) are all welcome in the trials. When he's six months old, any purebred can compete in Obedience, so long as he is not vicious, lame, completely blind or deaf. Thus, the emphasis is on brains; beauty, while appreciated, is secondary and really not important.

One of the sport's big lures for the average fancier is that it remains pure, or in the domain of the amateur. The A.K.C. does not license handlers for Obedience, and the professional seen in the ring with a dog other than his own is the exception and not the rule. Time spent in training and time spent at the trial itself make Obedience impractical and uneconomical for the pro. Nor are the clients there. Unless he is immobilized, the owner would rather train and handle his own dog. The nearest thing to a pro is a sort of a semipro, or an Obedience instructor.

So the amateur spirit prevails, and this extends to the six hundred judges who are licensed to judge for one or all of the four Obedience degrees. None works for a fee, and most are happy to have their travel and other necessary expenses covered. Obedience judging is an avocation in the purest sense, and there's no indication that it will ever be anything else.

Obedience judges are far more beloved than breed judges. Some are known as easy judges and some have the reputation of being difficult, but the sport's rules leave little room for personal interpretation and an easy judge grants only a few more points than a difficult one. So even a very sensitive man can be happy as an Obedience judge. He never attracts many critics, and the few he does attract seldom wish that he'd never been born.

The sport itself does have critics, and most of them are serious breeders who feel that Obedience lovers aren't doing anything to improve the breeds. "How many of those dogs could win in the breed ring?" is both their question and accusation. The answer is always "Some couldn't, some could, and some have."

Obviously, some of the Obedience dogs aren't eligible for the breed ring. Prior to 1936, these dogs had to stay at home. Now they can keep their owners happy. They can still participate in the dog game.

Of those eligible for the breed ring, some wouldn't stand much chance and some would. Their owners must decide, and some of them don't give a damn about making their dogs champions, just as many owners of champions don't give a damn about Obedience degrees.

But more and more champions are being seen in Obedience, a fact that pleases the veterans. In the beginning, it was thought that the owners of top show dogs would rush them into the new sport, as if to prove that canine beauty does not preclude brains. It happened all right, but the rush slowed down to a walk when noted dog fanciers, attuned to the easy training of show dogs, realized that it took more time, thinking, and patience to prepare their charges for the trials. The wealthier fanciers were interested, but most couldn't find trainers to handle their dogs. So they went back to the breed ring, where a man with a handler doesn't need to work and doesn't even have to be on speaking terms with his own dogs.

Fortunately, a new breed of fancier was waiting in the wings. It understood the true worth of the new sport and was willing to utilize God's gifts of time, intellect, and patience. So Obedience in America has never wavered. The chart shows a steady, spectacular growth: more trials every year, more fanciers and their dogs involved every year, more training clubs coming into existence every year. Along with the growth, more show dogs are being seen in Obedience, and more trial dogs are being seen in the breed ring. A decade ago, the average fancier was either all show or all trials. Today the dual fancier, one active with his dog(s) in both sports, is coming into his own. What the fancy really needs is more dual breeders, or ones who will breed with both conformation and brains in mind.

The strange thing about Obedience is that it hasn't caught fire with the general public. The man in the street still doesn't understand what it's all about. If he did, there would be no need for leash laws and other local ordinances pertaining to dogs that are now common throughout the country. Fewer dogs would dig up gardens, ruin valuable shrubbery, bite postmen, overturn garbage cans, and live their lives as nuisances. If only more dogs had a little training, more neighbors would be talking to neighbors.

The sport's nomenclature, simple as it is, soars above the layman's head. Even if he's a dog hater, or he's never been near a dog show, he's able to grasp some of the meaning of the title of champion. He understands that a champion dog is somehow superior to a nonchampion. But the Obedience degrees leaves him cold. To wit:

"Ever tell you about my Collie? He's a CD."

"A what?"

"A Companion Dog."

"Good. My dog is a real pal, too."

"My sister's Cocker is a CDX. X means excellent."

"Yes, some dogs are friendlier than others."

"She hopes to make him a Utility Dog."

"Really? Does she own some cows for him to herd?"

Try it on your doctor tomorrow. Tell him your dog is a UDT. He'll prescribe stronger medicine for you.

Just why the public is unaware of the sport and its virtues remains a puzzle, for Obedience has many levels and reaches into, or close to, every community in every state.

At the top, where the trials that count take place, is the same Big Time of the point show, plus the independent licensed events sponsored by training clubs, breed clubs, and specialty-show clubs.

A rung below are the match trials, which may or may not include breed judging. Here the trials are conducted in the Big Time's manner, but the results are unofficial. It's the rehearsal ground for the serious fancier and his dog. The A.K.C. rules and regulations apply, and the events are officially called sanctioned matches.

Next come the unsanctioned matches, usually sponsored by a newly formed local training club and sometimes open to mongrels. Basically, these clubs are out to promote the purebreds, but they are also interested in bettering canine-human relations in their communities, and all, including those who don't permit mongrels at their match trails, welcome them at their training classes.

For the serious fancier, the worth of the local club's offerings is in direct relation to the knowledge of the club's officers. But for every dog, some training is better than none, and there's no risk involved for the dog owner who doesn't intend to go on to the trials.

At pretty much the same level are 4-H club dog-training programs, adult-education classes, and programs sponsored by civic associations. At all of these, purebreds and mongrels are welcome.

Then, at a level and in a class by themselves are the hundreds of Obedience schools that have been springing up around the country. As the saying goes, this is where dog owners are trained to train their dogs. The trainers of both man and beast are usually experienced veterans of the sport, and a semester runs about eight weeks, with one session per week of an hour's duration in the early evening. Ten to twenty owners and their dogs constitute a class, and the tuition runs from fifteen to twenty-five dollars. Some of these schools accept mongrel students and some don't.

Unless the owner is an idiot, he and his dog cannot help but benefit from these schools. A dog more responsive to commands is always the result. And if the owner and his dog do their homework between classes, a well-trained student is the reward.

It is here, at the school level, that one can advance rapidly with his dog from simple training to the advanced training that actually prepares a dog for the trials. In our experience and observation, this is the place to start. Once he's broken to collar and lead, any dog of any age is ready. A young pup, of course, is sometimes too playful to take his work seriously, and we consider ten months early enough to begin his formal Obedience training. True, a pup of six months may compete at the formal trials, but getting him ready by that age is usually wishful thinking.

Now, despite the availability and economy of the training schools and training programs, many a fancier watches a few trials and decides to go it alone. It can be done. Helpful textbooks are in almost every public library. But it's the hard way. The easy way is to attend a training school with a record of success, do one's homework, attend a few trials to see how they are actually run, and then participate in a few match trials. When the dog is ready, go!

Almost always, the dogs who succeed at the trials were school trained. When home-trained dogs are successful, the owner usually admits that he learned his training methods at a school with another dog.

But whether he's school trained or home trained, the Obedience dog must first know and respond to the six basic commands: "Stand," "Heel," "Sit," "Stay," "Come," and "Down." Long before we qualified as fanciers, we taught our first dogs those commands. The dogs were such a pleasure to own that we decided the commands would make child rearing an easier task. So among the first words our offsprings learned were "Heel," "Sit," and "Stay." "Heel" came in handy when crossing a busy street or shopping, "Sit" often got them out of the way of adult traffic or the vacuum cleaner, and "Stay" kept them there. If it's any help, it takes less time to train a pup.

The six commands can be taught in any order, but we teach in the order named. We don't hurry the training, and find that once a pup has a couple of commands down pat, he learns the others in short order. Nor do we put much stock in a pup's memory, and we try to give him a command rehearsal each day. Sooner or later, whether he's headed for the Obedience trials or not, we start using his name before the command, as "Harry, Sit!" or "Harry, Come!" At home or in a trial, when Harry hears his name, he is alerted to the fact that he's about to do something. At our home, saying his name first also serves a peaceful purpose. When he hears "Harry, Come!" Harry comes, and five other Labs don't mount a charge.

The purists in Obedience insist that the dog's name should not be used before the command "Stay," for it is the only command that doesn't imply motion of some kind. Using his name, then, will alert him to doing nothing and thus confuse him. Well, that's a pretty fine point, and it credits the canine with a sensitive mind that he probably doesn't possess. We can look at one of our dogs and say, "Listen, you bum, Stay!" and he stays. Never any confusion.

Once the dog has the six commands stored in his brain, he's capable of being trained to win his first Obedience degree. There are four such degrees, and usually a dog picks them up in the following order:

1.) *Companion Dog*, known in the sport as a CD. The equivalent, in human education, to a diploma from elementary school.
2.) *Companion Dog Excellent*, or CDX. A high-school diploma.
3.) *Utility Dog*, or UD. A college degree, either B.A. or B.S.
4.) *Tracking Dog*, or TD. An M.A.

The first three degrees must be won in the order named. The TD can be won at any time. Thus it is possible for a dog to earn his master's degree before entering the first grade. Dogs who accomplish this remain unaware of their feat and continue to treat their masters as equals.

The dog who earns all four degrees is entitled to wear the initials UDT (Utility Dog Tracking) after his name. Obedience can pay him no higher honor. Luv Uvmy Life, UDT has to be a dog of high intelligence. Ch. Luv Uvyr Life, UDT has no more worlds to conquer.

To the distress of the dog fancy, animal researchers have not yet discovered that Obedience trials are fine research laboratories. If they ever do, the debate over animal intelligence will end, and loyal supporters of the elephant, ape, and cat will be put to rout. Indeed, those learned souls who belittle anthropomorphism would have second thoughts if they could find time to observe a few UDT dogs in action. All of a dog's senses, instincts and lessons aren't enough to guide him to success. There are times when he must do some heavy thinking on his own, and he does, and he's obviously elated when he succeeds.

With the exception of TD, the Obedience degrees must be won in the Big Time by earning a qualifying score or better under three different judges at three different trials. Each qualifying score is a leg, and three legs make a degree.

The dog is always shooting for 200, or perfection. It's a rare

The Long Down tests a dog's patience. He may move his head or tail a bit, but any other body movement is penalized. In this photo, none of the dogs shows an inclination to break.　*Louise Branch*

achievement; the great majority of Obedience judges have never granted that high a score and never will. But the dogs are unaware of that fact. They try, and if they make 170, they qualify, or earn a leg. *If*, that is.

A dog can score as high as 184 in a CD trial and still not qualify, and that's where the big IF comes in. The dog must score at least half the points allotted to each exercise. So IF he goofs just once by scoring 14 points in a 30-point exercise, he has disqualified himself, no matter his final score. Here's a look at how CD is scored:

1.)	Heel on Leash	35 points
2.)	Stand for Examination	30 points
3.)	Heel Free	45 points
4.)	Recall	30 points
5.)	Long Sit (one minute)	30 points
6.)	Long Down (three minutes)	30 points
	TOTAL (possible)	200 points

The dog and his handler work as a single act during the first four exercises. If they are in complete harmony, 140 points result.

The Long Sit at a Boxer Specialty. Thus far, all of the dogs appear to be qualifying, but some will be docked points for extremely sloppy sits. *William P. Gilbert*

Five and six are group exercises, limited to no more than fifteen handlers and their dogs. Now, assuming that Buster gets through the first five exercises in perfect form, he has 170 and his handler is a nervous wreck. One more exercise to go, and they are shooting for the rare 200 and all the loot. Obedience usually offers more trophies, prizes, and cash than the breed ring.

Now the final exercise, the Long Down, begins. The dogs and their handlers are all in line, facing the judge. In the official prose of the A.K.C.: "The handlers, on order from the judge, will down their dogs without touching the dogs or their collars." On order, the handlers march across the ring, turn, and face their dogs. After three minutes, the handlers march back to their dogs. "The dogs must stay in the down position until after the judge says, 'Exercise finished.' "

What happened during the three minutes is what usually happens. Buster, still a pup and full of fun, became bored and decided to play with the Puli next to him. The Puli responded by sitting up and licking Buster. And down the line, a Greyhound anxious to make friends struggled to his feet and trotted their way. Net result: three goofs.

It could be argued in court that only Buster was guilty. But in Obedience, all three are judged guilty and disqualified. Guilt by association, yes, but still guilt. So all three blew their chances for a leg, the loot, and a happy ride home.

So among other qualities, a trial dog must be steady or have an iron will. He must keep his mind on the business at hand, forget the other dogs, and not be distracted by what's happening elsewhere. The tensions felt in the breed ring by the handlers, if not the dogs, are as nothing compared to Obedience, where the unexpected is commonplace. Outside the ring and within a few feet of the working dog or dogs, distractions occur with maddening frequency: a woman spectator screams at her child, a loose dog runs by, people shout greetings to each other, a three-year-old escapes from Mama and toddles into the ring and toward a dog, somebody falls over a chair, cheers and applause and whistles award a winning dog in another ring, or lightning streaks through dark clouds. The trial dog is curious, forgets what he's doing, and makes a mistake. Disqualified. Too bad. Weeks of training have gone down the drain because of one simple, idiotic, unavoidable happening.

Although the exceptional dog who scores a 200 and all the others who bear the laurels of UD and UDT are theoretical champions in their field, the actual title "champion" does not exist in Obedience.* The small segment of the general public that is aware of the sport finds this confusing, as do some fanciers and dog editors. Within recent memory, *The New York Times* profiled a lady dog fancier who had been exhibiting Briards for some ten years. After some success in the breed ring, she decided it would be nice to own a dual champion. In due time, her champion bitch earned a CD degree, and to this day the lady and *The Times* may believe that she owns a dual champion. Is it possible to question what one reads in *The Times?*

Yes. A dual champion always was and still remains a dog with both a breed championship and a field-trial championship to his

---

* Although it did in the beginning when the CD degree meant Champion Dog. The breed devotees objected, and the C was changed to Companion.

credit. Field-trial champions come only from the ranks of the Sporting and Hound breeds.

"Who says you can't teach an old dog new tricks?" asked the lady in *The Times*. It seems that her champion bitch was over six when she started in Obedience. Well, it would be difficult to find anyone in Obedience who would say such a thing. Our oldest successful student was over twelve when she started her home-training course in CD. Three weeks and twelve training hours later, she earned a first leg with a score of 191.

Now, anyone with an Obedience background will tell you that three weeks of home training crowned by success the first time out is pretty nice going, especially when the trainers are rank amateurs. We did it as an experiment to prove, to our own satisfaction anyway, that the canine can learn things through observation.

Folly, the twelve-year-old student, had known her basic commands for years. But the interesting plus that she had going for her was the fact that she had watched several other dogs go through their Obedience training at home. Indeed, she had often played a role in the training, in that she and another dog would

Disaster strikes during a training session at the Sportsman's Dog Training Club of Detroit. Moments later, all of the dogs shown sitting were breaking.

sit and act as poles for the figure-eight exercise. At other times, as when a dog was being trained for his leash and free-heeling exercises, she'd trot along a couple of feet from his left. After a while, whenever the dog stopped and sat, she'd do likewise.

In training for the group exercises, the Long Sit and the Long Down, we usually put the student between a couple of experienced dogs. At the trials, he's going to have a dog on each side of him, so he might as well get used to it early. Well, if Folly was around, she'd join the trio of her own accord.

So Folly, through her personal observations, sort of trained herself for the CD. All we really had to do was polish her performance through corrections. Recall was the only exercise that caused any trouble. She'd come all right, but at first she'd forget to sit and go to heel immediately. Correcting that little detail took up a great deal of the training time. It was as if she wanted us to work for a change.

That was our second solid experience with the power of canine observation. The first happened some years ago with the Samoyed named Butch. From his kennel run, he had a fine view of a field where we trained our Labs who were headed for the field trials. So he observed quite a few dogs retrieving thrown dummies from both land and water, and after about the third one he didn't watch quietly. His bark was loud and sharp and provided an unappreciated musical background to the training sessions. This went on for a couple of years. Finally, we recognized that he wanted to join the action. So we started him on a dummy, and right from the start he would retrieve it to hand from land or water. Butch wasn't steady and he had a hard mouth, but otherwise he was a pretty fair retriever, trained by himself through observation. He was a show champ, and if we could have doctored him to look like a Lab, maybe we could have turned him into a dual champion and confused *The Times'* man even more.

To return to our subject (a five-word device that dog fancier Terhune used frequently in his writings), the Tracking Dog degree is the only one that does not require three legs, and the only one not held at the trials. It is a one-shot affair, always held far afield over territory as virgin as possible, and with two judges in attendance.

The dog, without assistance of any kind from his handler, tracks a trail laid by a stranger and then finds a small article hidden by the stranger. The trail is never less than 440 yards. It's always tricky, and always known to the judges. There's no time limit for completing the task, so long as the dog is obviously working at tracking. A dog either passes or fails this test. If he fails, he needs more training before he has another go at the TD.

The canine nose is all important, of course, and that's the reason why the Hound and Sporting breeds do so well in tracking. But Poodles, German Shepherds, Doberman Pinschers, Collies, and Shetland Sheepdogs are also TD stars. Our betters, as the chapter up ahead will reveal, insist that any breed can be trained to track. Owners of Boxers, Pugs, Bulldogs, Pekingese, Japanese Spaniels, and French Bulldogs will be happy to hear that news.

The big thing to remember when training any dog of any age is that he is not as intelligent as you are. Try as he will, he's never going to read books or understand languages. We, the superior animals, can't do anything about increasing his brain-power, but we can help him attain his maximum potential.

His field of vision is greater than ours, but he's color blind, and he doesn't see as clearly. Otherwise, all of his senses are keener than ours, and all of his instincts are stronger. The trick is to channel those senses and instincts into a training program, and that isn't difficult. Repeat a word, a sound, or a signal often enough as you direct or haul him through a given action, and sooner or later he'll learn the meaning of the word, sound, or signal. He puts one and one together and learns through association. Praised and rewarded, he does a little better the next time. His natural instinct for the good things in life comes into play. Like man, he's a social animal and aims to please. If he doesn't, he's an ungrateful bum and doesn't understand his own kind.

Friends may laugh, but we think collar association is a big help in training a dog. Each of our dogs wears a collar night and day. This is changed only when a training session is about to begin. On goes a lightweight choke collar. After a few sessions, the dog senses what the collar means: school is in session, and it's time for him to concentrate, or whatever dogs do as a substitute. So the regular collar means loafing, and the special collar means working. Later, at the trials, the training collar means that he's about to go to work. There is no sure way of proving this theory, of course, but it has always worked with our dogs. At the very least, it gives us confidence, and perhaps our confidence runs down the leash to the dogs. If nervousness can, why not confidence? For both training and the trials, incidentally, we use a plain snap-on work lead.

As mentioned, the Obedience dog must know the six basic commands. All of his exercises are based on them. "Stand" (stance) and "Heel" (gait) have been covered. Here's how we go about training the other four commands on the home grounds:

Sit! The command is "Harry, Sit!" Note that there should always be a slight pause between the dog's name and the command word. First, get the dog's attention. Then, tell him what to do. It is thus with all verbal commands.

Have the dog standing at heel position. Hold the leash tight, this time in the right hand.

On the command, tug up on the leash and push down with the left hand on the dog's quarters. The human action is simultaneous.

The average pup or dog, no matter how big, is going to sit. A big, stubborn lunk may not. In that case, overdo the tug with the right hand and whack the dog's rear with the left. He'll sit.

Most canine students will get the idea after a half dozen attempts, and the down action on his rear can be discontinued. For the next couple of sessions, just the verbal command and the tug on the leash will suffice.

This is the right time to observe just how the dog sits, and to correct him if necessary. In Obedience, he must sit straight and square, with forelegs even and firm and hind legs tight and under him. It is not a natural sit for every dog and always bears watching. Some will sit on the end of the spine, with both hindlegs on one side. Others go in for the debutante slouch and sort of lean to one side. And then there are the ones who plant their forefect wide, as if drunk and trying to find a center of gravity.

Any dog can be taught to sit properly, just on the verbal command, within three short training sessions. If not, the trainer can't lick his grandmother.

Once a dog has learned how to sit like a gentleman on command, we combine this with his heeling. In all of Obedience's heel exercises, the dog must sit at heel (without command) every time the handler stops. So now we blend the heeling and sitting, and begin with the dog on leash.

Now the leash is in the left hand. The handler walks along with the dog at heel position. The handler stops, and tugs back and up as he stops. Ninety percent of the time, the dog trained to sit will sit. But if he belongs to the 10 percent, then the verbal command to sit should accompany the tug. After about three training sessions, the dullest student will stop and sit without verbal command or tug. Then it's just a matter of practice to get him to sit properly off leash.

Stay! The command is "Stay!" if you're a purist, or "Harry, Stay!" if you're not.

This can be taught any number of ways, but we've found the easiest method is to have the dog off leash and sitting at heel position. As the handler gives the command, he does two other things: steps ahead, leading off with right foot, and swings left arm in a backward arc, so that the open left palm of hand almost touches dog's nose.

The handler should not be surprised if the dog stays right where he is, for the left palm is a sort of stop sign and deterrent. Half the dogs in America will react that way, and lavish praise should be immediate. But during the first few sessions, the dog should not be expected to stay where he is forever. A few seconds at a time, building up to about thirty seconds, is sufficient at this stage.

What about the dogs who pop up and start to follow despite

the verbal command and the swinging palm? The handler, being close, simply grabs the dog's collar, makes him sit, and lectures him. Immediate restraint is necessary, but not punishment.

Sooner or later, if only to avoid that yank on his collar, the dog will stay at sit. Then if he's praised or given a tidbit, he'll get the general idea in a hurry.

Note that this is the first time in a pup's or a dog's training that we use a hand signal. If the canine is headed for the Obedience trials, hand signals are in his future, and this is a simple one for him to learn. Also, if he's a house pet, the "Stay" command, verbal or hand signal or both, comes in handy. It keeps him where he is when he's about to enter the house with muddy paws, or you want him to stay in the kitchen, or you don't want him to walk across a freshly painted floor.

As time goes on, the dog stays put every time he sees the open palm of either hand swinging toward him.

Come! The command is "Harry, Come!" and the dog is supposed to do just that. Again, we teach this one off leash.

The dog is commanded to sit and stay. The handler wanders off about twenty feet, faces the dog, and gives the "Come" command. Half the time the dog will just sit there.

If the dog comes, the antic is repeated over and over. No problem.

If the dog doesn't come, the handler keeps repeating the command and makes it enticing by clapping his hands, getting down on his knees, slapping his legs, or running off. The stupidest dog in creation will not be able to resist running to such a silly human being. However, if he's the exception, wave a sirloin steak. When he does come, congratulations are generous, and the practice runs continue.

Well, that's the way we do it, and we're probably wrong, but our dogs don't realize it. In almost all Obedience classes, the command is taught on leash. The handler stands out in front of the sitting dog, gives the command, and snaps on the leash. If this doesn't work, the handler stands closer to the dog, gives a more violent snap on the command, and steps backward, yanking if he must. So the dog is sort of forced to come along, and learns to do so.

The leash method calls for less imagination and is not as much fun, but it's a good one, and guess what? When the dog arrives, a slight tug on the leash reminds him to sit facing his handler. This is something a dog at the trials must know.

Of course, teaching him to sit on arrival can be taught off leash, simply by giving him the "Sit" command when he arrives. Maybe it takes longer. We don't know.

Down! The command is "Harry, Down!" and teaching it is a one- or two-step program but never a problem.

The dog is at sit position, the handler crouching before him and facing him. As he gives the verbal command, the handler lifts the dog's forelegs and the dog must go down. Often, ten or twelve such exercises are all a dog needs, and he'll go down on command without having his legs touched. But if he doesn't go down on command in the first training session, chances are that step two should be invoked the next time.

This calls for the leash. The handler stands in front of the sitting dog, facing him and with the leash looped to the left hand. The bottom of the loop should be about two inches above ground level.

On the command, the handler steps on the loop with his right foot and down goes the dog. It won't hurt the dog, but a handler who feels that treatment is rough can step on the loop and bear down slowly. This method, repeated frequently and interlaced with praise and tidbits, will teach any dog to go down on command within a couple of sessions. In the case of a dullard, the handler can also use his free hand to push down on the dog's back.

In the case of step two, this is also a handy time to teach the "Down" hand signal. As the handler gives the command and steps on the leash, he raises his right arm into the position of a policeman stopping traffic.

It has been said that this is the most important hand signal of all for the modern dog to understand. Presumably, as a dog is about to run in front of a truck, his master gives the hand signal and the dog drops in his tracks, saving his own life. Conditions, of course, have to be ideal. The dog, for example, must be watching his master.

But even for the dog not headed for Obedience, this command, by voice or by hand, is a useful one. It keeps a dog on a rug when you don't want him on your lap, or it keeps him from jumping up on the visiting minister, or it saves the Christmas goose that's waiting to be carved.

Most of our own adult dogs learn to go down when we point to the floor. They are not trained to do this, and seem to pick it up from one another. Either that, or it's forefinger telepathy.

The conscientious reader will have noted that we teach a couple of hand signals along with the verbal commands. Many owners teach each hand signal with all commands, or all six.

There's nothing wrong with teaching the six signals along with the six basics, except that overall training takes a little longer, and in our human-animal setup the sooner a pup learns his basics, the less trouble for us. We happen to teach the "Stay" and "Down" commands early because no extra work is involved and they are handy around the house. The other signals are taught as leisure time permits. Once a dog knows a verbal command, using the proper hand signals with it will soon bring results. Association.

Here are the four signals we teach in relaxed manner:

Sit! Left elbow held close to body, with forearm swinging up and extended toward dog as if offering a plate of food. Left palm up. Fingers flip up.

It may see odd, but the easiest way to teach this signal is with the dog in a down position and on leash. The handler stands close, facing dog, holding leash short in right hand. On the verbal command to sit, the leash is tugged up. To do this, the forearm must swing up, which is the hand signal in the rough.

Unless the dog has the neck of a bull, he will sit up. After that, the usual practice makes perfect, and finally the verbal command is eliminated.

If the dog does not sit up on the command, the handler must invent supplemental actions. It sometimes helps to step toward the dog while tugging up. Most dogs don't want to be stepped on and will sit up. Or the handler can poke the dog's chest with his foot.

Once a dog obeys a hand signal to sit up from a down position, the same signal will bring him to a sit from a standing position. In the case of the unusual dog who defies this general rule, it's back to the leash again, and a second party is called in. The dog stands, the handler tugs up on the leash as he gives the signal, and the assistant slaps the dog's rump. The unusual dog soon learns that the hand signal means both sit up and sit down.

Stand! The left hand dropped at the side, palm open and facing rear, is the hand signal for "Stand." Palm students will be quick to note that this is just a modification of the "Stay" signal.

It is taught with the dog standing at heel position, and the palm right in front of the dog's nose every time the verbal command is given. Over a period of time, the hand moves back, actually touching the dog along his side. After a while, the dog learns that the handler's stiff left arm means "Stand."

This is a little trickier than it reads, especially for the dog who has been trained to sit in the heel position whenever the handler isn't moving. The dog who sits is confused and requires immediate correction.

This signal is not necessary for Obedience until a dog is going for his UD, so it's not an important one in early training. When he's standing, the regular "Stay" signal will keep him standing. Nor does the "Stand" signal have any particular value around the house. Not in our house, anyway.

Come! The right hand starts at the side and curves in an upward arc in front of the body, ending somewhere between the left elbow and shoulder. It is pretty much the same as the cave man's signal of "Come hither, my love."

The dog who doesn't learn this through association with the verbal command goes back to the leash. A long leash, maybe twenty feet in length, or a rope will do. The leash is held in the left hand and a little high. On the verbal command, the right hand swoops in an arc, grabs the leash, and yanks. Now the dog comes, and in time he learns what that swooping right hand means.

Sometimes, a fun-loving pup who has the verbal command down pat will become confused or amused by the hand signal. If he's off leash, he may run in the opposite direction. If the handler chases him, it's not fatal, but a lot of training may have gone down the drain. The wise handler keeps repeating the verbal command and trying to coax the pup back to him. Shouting and running in the opposite direction from the pup often helps.

Heel! This is another of the hand signals that is of no particular value until a dog goes into the UD trials. Then he must know two hand signals.

The first signal starts him walking at heel. Just a forward swinging motion of the left hand as the handler steps off on his left foot.

The other is the reverse, or a swinging motion of the left hand from front to left side. It brings the dog from in front of the handler to his left side.

The easiest way of teaching is through association with the verbal command, and by UD time it's no problem. Unless one lives in an overcrowded ballroom, the signals are of no value around the house.

Hand signals, while an important part of Obedience work are not regulated. The ones found on these pages are the usual ones, but there's no law against inventing your own. Anything goes, so long as the dog obeys.

There are certain truisms about training that pertain to almost all dogs, whatever the goal in mind. The trainer should be patient and understanding and try to realize that his canine student is not his intellectual equal, no matter how much he paid for the dog.

And a dog comes along faster in his training if his teacher is one person. If all members of a family shout commands at a dog as soon as he learn them, the dog's reaction will be as a strange driver's to traffic signs in Boston. There's plenty of time for the rest of the family to get into the act, but never a time for relatives, friends, and neighbors. And always, always, only the trainer handles the dog in actual Obedience exercises.

Tone of voice is always stressed in training tomes. Actually, it is overstressed, for it's next to impossible for a person always to use the same tone when uttering commands. Dogs are neither delicate nor extremely sensitive, and the command voice can cover a wide range of tones. The tone should be firm and sound like business, as when a woman asks her husband for the seventh time to remove his junk from the basement. So the tone should be stronger than saccharine and less than frightening. Vocal volume is unimportant and bellowing unnecessary, thanks to the canine's fine audio sense. When you whisper a command in a quiet room, and the dog fails to respond, he's lazy or faking or both. A whack on his rump is indicated.

It is a legend of our time that punishment is best applied via a rolled newspaper, but by the time the owner finds, rolls, and employs the newspaper, the dog has forgotten how he erred and the punishment represents wasted energy. A slap over the dog's quarters with open palm is a quick, handy way to get the message across and on time. The slap doesn't have to be severe. In the case of the big breeds, a mighty slap will only hurt the hand and leave the dog laughing.

We know of only one dog fancier, a lady professional handler, who advocates socking a dog across his muzzle with rolled newspaper, yardstick, or any other handy item. "That's the way we handled the kids when I worked at the orphanage," she told us. Some of her dogs are shy and cringe, and others bite.

For our money, the open palm over the rear serves the purpose. It adds the right touch of emphasis to unprintable words when a house dog is found upon a bed, for example. We are aware that the best-trained dogs will, on occasion, test their masters. Perhaps there is such a thing as a canine sense of humor. But under our roof, beasts are not allowed upon our beds. It is a matter of equal rights. We do not sleep on their beds.

Every dog should, of course, have his own name, even if it's only Dog. The name is vital in his training, but as time goes on and the dog forms an association with a voice or voices—in the way he can tell the sound of the family's auto from that of a stranger's—just one name becomes unimportant. Thumper, one of our best-known Labs, is an old man now and one of several house dogs. Dumper Do, Dewey, Meathead, Hey You, Drop It, Lunkhead, and Choir Boy are a few of his other names at home, and he responds to all. Then there's his half-sister Chub, who responds to Chubby, Cha Cha, Mafia, Speed, Lady Godiva, and Hells Bells. Daughter Cary trained her for Obedience. When Chub was going for her second leg in CD, Cary used a different name for the bitch on each command. Chub qualified for the leg with a 193. Only the judge was confused. Of course, if we're in a hurry, we get confused now and then. "Lady Godiva, Come," will always bring Chub when we want Duchess, who is also Lady Bird.

With almost any dog, training becomes easier as time marches on. If he's not abused, the dog will learn lesson five faster than he learned lesson four, and ten more quickly than nine. Meanwhile, he may forget lesson two unless it is reviewed with him once in a while.

A dog who will respond to many names (just sounds to him) has no trouble learning that a variety of sounds mean the same thing. "Chub, Sit!," for example, will cause her to sit. So will the word "Pow," or one snap of the fingers. She will go down on the word "Bang," or two snaps of the fingers. In less than a couple of minutes, now that she's an old-timer, she could be taught the meaning of a sound or a silent signal. Since the dog isn't looking one's way, we prefer the sound commands around the house. This has saved us a few broken necks, both canine and human. A pup or young dog will often bark or decide to dash ahead of his master when the phone rings. In our house, the canines are trained to stay where they are and keep their big mouths shut when the telephone rings. We no longer risk our lives trying to get to the phone at two in the morning.

Obviously, Rover could be trained to sit on the command "Rover, Fly!" We've never witnessed that at any Obedience trial, but there's nothing in the rules to prevent it. Nor is there any rule that says a command must be given in English. At trials held near and in Canada, one often hears commands given in French. At many trials in this country, it's common to watch a dog obeying comands in German, Italian, Spanish, and other tongues. So long as the dog performs his exercises, the judge isn't concerned with the handler's language. Thus, if the judge is not up on his Spanish, what sounds to him like the command to sit could be freely translated as "Pedro, Sit! Or I'll boil you in oil when we get home." If Pedro has been taught what "boiled in oil" means, he'll sit in record time.

One of the safest training generalizations relates to the trainer. It's always best to skip training when one isn't in the mood for it, not feeling well, or at odds with the world. A man should not fight with his wife and then go outdoors and train his dog. If he wants to do both things on the same day, he should train his dog first and then fight with his wife.

And so we come to a popular question of first-time owners: "Why should I train my pup? All I want him to be is a good pet."

Come, come. Why train the child? A good pet doesn't occur by accident or natural inheritance. Untrained, the pup, like the child, becomes a juvenile delinquent.

Still, many a mother of properly raised, solid citizens finds the training of a puppy beyond her ken. They may have read this adage of the dog game: "It is one and a half times more trouble to raise and train a puppy than a child." False and ridiculous. Listen, we could raise and train five hundred more puppies with ease, but raising and training one more child would drive us crazy.

Unfortunately for many owners, a pup isn't whelped fully trained. But if his future doesn't include training, then he is whelped to live a life of boredom, and a bored dog spells trouble, nuisance, and pest. So far as a dog is concerned, the more training the merrier, and the better his chances of leading a full life with man.

Training a dog to be a worthwhile pet is very little trouble.

Training him to be a show dog takes little extra effort. Training him for the Obedience trials takes a hell of a lot of effort.

Of course, it may not seem that way when one is a spectator at the trials. The dog is older and weighs more than the little girl who is putting him through his paces, and somebody's grandmother is handling a pup of seven months. The sport knows no age limits and proves that a sure empathy can exist between man and canine.

Whether they ever go to a dog show or an Obedience trial or not, most dogs are house pets and lead pretty empty lives, in the sense that they don't do a damn thing to earn their keep. They eat, sleep, wag tails, ask for attention, and bark at strangers. Not much of a life.

The trained dog, at least, is asked to do something once in a while, if only to obey a command. And he can also be of some help around the house. To his obvious satisfaction, by the way.

That's why we always teach a seventh basic command, or "Fetch." It's a command a dog must know for the Open (CDX) trials anyway, where he must (1) retrieve a tossed dumbbell on the flat, and (2) retrieve a tossed dumbbell over a high jump.

Around our house, the command has two meanings: a plain carry, or go get something and carry it back, or retrieve. When we come home from shopping, a couple of dogs carry small packages into the house. Or if one of us in the basement needs a hammer, a shout inspires somebody upstairs to give a dog a hammer and send him down the stairs. Those are plain carries.

Our mail is delivered around noon. The rural postman honks his horn, a door is opened for a dog, and the dog retrieves the mail. At eventide, a "Thumper, fetch slippers," will have him bringing the slippers from the bedroom. Both of them. Moor Born makes two trips. At any time, a "Folly, Fetch" and a pointed finger will have her retrieving something from the floor. We've never needed a butler or a maid.

Well, it may sound foolish, but the dogs seem to enjoy doing things and the command saves us a couple of hundred miles of walking every year. Labs, of course, are natural retrievers, but any dog can be taught to fetch.

Teaching is easiest when the student is still a pup and looking for play. He'll chase a small ball, pick it up, and carry it back to the tosser. If he runs off with it, a long leash or a length of rope is the remedy. The next time he runs off with the ball, just haul him in.

Our eighth basic command is "Kennel." It means the dog is supposed to enter something, as indicated by a wave of the hand. Thus, a command of "Kennel" sends a dog into a car, into a crate, into the house, into a room, or into the kennel.

And it meant the same thing to our daughters when they were pups.

It is of no use in Obedience.

CHAPTER IX

OBEDIENCE: TIPS FROM THE TOP

Helpful Advice from America's Leading Practitioners and Enthusiasts of Obedience: Bill Watkins and the Amazing Dudley, Professional Info from Kae Reiley, Judge Sam Gardner's Bulldogs and Views, and Dual Fancier Corinne Macdonald and Her Schipperkes ⸹ Values for Show Dogs

IN THE annals of the sport, there's never been a true story to top the one about a roofing contractor names Bill Watkins and a stray pup he named Dudley. The tale has a thousand versions, and one or more are repeated whenever three Obedience devotees meet, but here are the facts as Bill told them to us:

It all began more than a decade ago when Bill surprised both himself and his wife by presenting her with a living Christmas present: an Airedale pup. Neither of them knew anything about dogs or the dog game and, like most first-time owners, did nothing to increase their knowledge. Both assumed that the pup would mature into a fine pet, but what he grew into was a holy terror. The friendly beast had failed to train himself and proved unmanageable.

Then a friend found a half-starved, stray pup. He was unable to keep the pup himself and asked Bill to hold the little black orphan for a couple of weeks while an attempt was made to find the owner. By the time it was apparent that the rightful owner wasn't going to step forward, Bill and his wife had grown fond of the pup. They adopted him and named him Dudley in honor of another friend's black dog.

The sentimental decision to add a new member to the family proved costly. Their vet found all sorts of things wrong with Dudley, although nothing that he couldn't cure. He figured the pup was three to four months old and, despite the long tail, might be a Poodle. So the pup's tail was docked. If they were going to own a Poodle, Bill and Helen wanted a proper Poodle.

But no matter the newcomer's breed, this time they were determined to have a trained dog. The responsibility was Bill's, and he had only to look at the Airedale to realize that roofing doesn't help a man to train a dog. So he joined a local dog training club.

Dudley was the youngest canine at the training sessions. But he proved to be the star of the class, so great a star that a couple of other owners suggested formal Obedience training. Bill didn't know what they were talking about, but he was enjoying the work as much as his pup and figured they had nothing to lose. So Bill started asking questions, located an Obedience training school within easy driving distance, and signed up for a ten-week course.

Training sessions were held once a week. At the end of the fourth week, the professional instructor took Bill aside and suggested that Dudley was ready for the Novice (CD) class at a match trial. Bill had never heard of a match trial either. Or of a dog show. It doesn't seem possible, for he hadn't been born yesterday. Still, he wasn't a sporting man, and claims he never read the sport pages.

So Dudley, now about six months old, went to his first match trial, turned in the highest score, and went home with all the loot. He went to five more match trials and was highest scorer in two of those.

By then, everyone was urging Bill to try Dudley in the Big Time. All that stood in the way was the American Kennel Club. There was no chance of locating the pup's papers, and the A.K.C.

The great Dudley demonstrates his current form in two Open exercises: Retrieve over High Jump (above) and Broad Jump. *Rosamond Hart*

Proving that he's only canine, Dudley goofs the bar jump, a Directed Jumping exercise in Utility. If this had occurred at an actual trial, Obedience fans would have gone into mourning. *Helen Watkins*

would have to list him as a Poodle before he could compete. Some will say it was a miracle, but the listing was accomplished in six weeks, and Dudley was ready to go.

More than ready, as it turned out. He won his CD degree with ease, scoring better than 195 on each of the three successive legs.

News travels fast in the Obedience world. The sport's enthusiasts started watching the record of Bill and Dudley. Who was this new guy? What was the Poodle's breeding? Would the team fall on its collective face in the more difficult CDX trials?

Old-timers say that a sigh of relief was heard from coast to coast when Dudley disqualified himself on his try for a second CDX leg. It proved that Dudley was only canine, and that Watkins was only human. They, too, could make mistakes. Owners looked more kindly on their dogs and themselves. You can't win every time.

But Bill and Dudley came close to disproving that theory. The gray* Poodle stands at twenty-two inches, he was a UD holder at about eighteen months, and in his career he retired every worthwhile trophy (three wins) around. Bill retired him after six years of campaigning, but one of these days he intends to bring the old man back for the Tracking degree. Fans hope that he does. Dudley, UDT. That would be fitting for the dog whom Obedience authority Sam Gardner calls the Einstein of dogdom.

Veterans of the dog game claim that Obedience will never see another dog the equal of Dudley. Ten times in his career, the wonder Poodle scored a perfect 200! It's a rare feat, and the dog who achieves it just once is considered something close to immortal.

Of course, the dog is only half the story in Obedience. The other half is the trainer and handler. In this case, Bill Watkins.

He claims he doesn't have a bag of tricks, that there's nothing unusual about his training methods, and that he still has a lot to learn. Nobody believes him, but that's what the man says. Everyone who knows him agrees, however, that there is a Watkins

---

* It's not unusual for a black puppy coat to end up gray.

Theory of Dog Training, and that it can be applied by every owner, whether his dog is headed for Obedience or improved social manners. We read the Theory this way:

> *A time to train.* The time is anytime, but not when one is tired, angry, frustrated, ill, hurried, or otherwise not one's lovable self.
>
> *A way to train.* Take it easy. Don't press the dog, don't be hard on him. The dog is a child and should be treated like one.
>
> *The thinking man.* All dogs cannot be trained successfully by a set method. What works with one may not work with another. So training must be flexible and requires some thought. There are really no problem dogs, just limited-thinking masters.
>
> *Follow-through.* Once the dog learns a command, he must always obey it. When he is disobedient, take the time to correct him then and there. If he's capable of learning something, he's capable enough of doing it again.
>
> *Spoiling.* There's no harm in spoiling a dog, so long as it doesn't go too far and doesn't offend the master. Bill's dogs sleep on his bed, for example, but they are not allowed on other furniture, and are not permitted to beg at the table.
>
> *Obedience training.* Eight to ten months of age is about right for most pups. Dudley was started earlier, of course, but the Dudleys are the exceptions.
>
> *Rapport.* If you can't establish this with your dog, forget Obedience.

The theory is a proved one, for the Bill Watkins success story in Obedience started with Dudley and continues today with his other Poodle stars. We find ourselves in agreement, even unto the spoiling business, something most dog owners won't admit and feel a bit guilty about. We do not, however, go for the sleeping-on-the-bed bit. Nor does Bill's wife, for that matter. But she permits it, and it may be her theory that husbands should be spoiled a little, too.

Since Dudley's retirement, Bill has remained with Poodles, a breed he considers made in heaven for Obedience. He is not inter-

Coach Bill Watkins gives his Obedience team a few pointers after a practice session on the home grounds. Dudley, now retired, shows the most interest. *Rosamond Hart*

ested in breeding or showing, or—for that matter—in Airedales. Since stray Poodles of Dudley's intelligence are in short supply, he found his current stars as pups at Kaely Kennels in the East.

The small kennel is owned by Kae Reiley, a breeder of all three varieties—and one of the land's leading teachers of Obedience. She is a protégé of the late Blanche Saunders, the woman who did so much to popularize Obedience in this country and the author of almost all of the early worthwhile literature on the subject. Long ago, Miss Saunders tried to interest us in the sport and failed. Our unfortunate impression of the activity had been garnered at dog shows where little, garden-club-type ladies shouted commands at small dogs in a tone and velocity of speech that a general of seven armies would have envied. Years later, and through Miss Reiley, we became curious and finally involved. Evidence of the sport's benefits were all around us: so many hapless owners of idiot dogs had become, almost overnight, happy owners of obedient dogs. Same people, same dogs.

Technically, there are no professionals in Obedience. The closest would be the Obedience-school instructors who teach others how to train their dogs. For reasons unknown to science, the average owner feels he can't turn out a well-trained dog. He does, however, respond to group therapy, and that's one of the real reasons for the phenomenal growth of the schools.

So Kae Reiley, one of our leading instructors, is a sort of professional by inference. She is also what she was in the beginning, a dog fancier, and continues to handle her own dogs with marked success in trials held in this country, Canada, and Bermuda. And since she's a Poodle breeder, she sticks with that breed. With all those credentials, plus a roomful of trophies, it's reasonable to assume that she's not revealing all she knows on these pages, but just enough to whet the appetite for more.

She's a firm believer in an early training start, and begins teaching the basic commands to her own pups when they are eight or nine weeks old. Indeed, she has been doing this for more than twenty years, which puts her about a dozen years ahead of the canine experts who decided, after observing tens of thousands of pups under controlled conditions, that the average pup starts using his brain in a positive manner at about eight weeks of age. Thus Kae starts stuffing a pup's brain with respect for authority before it becomes cluttered with a bunch of nonsense desires, such as chewing shoes, digging up gardens, and antiquing contemporary furniture legs. Most pups are happy little creatures at two months, so she keeps the training on the fun level, is lavish with her praise and not stingy about offering tidbits as rewards. There's no training schedule, and sessions are held as time permits. The sessions are always brief, and always stopped short of canine boredom. And since the pups she retains are all headed for Obedience, all are taught to retrieve small objects. The dog who can't retrieve will never make his CDX, so Kae gets over that hurdle in a hurry. Every pup in the world will chase and pick up some tossed object: a small dumbbell, a brightly colored ball, a rolled sock, or a nylon bone. By the time he learns to pick up the object and retrieve it to hand, he also knows a new command: "Fetch!"

The informal, fun training continues through the third and fourth month, and then Kae eases up for a few weeks. This is the period when the student is losing his milk (puppy) teeth, he resents the slight discomfort, and may even suspect that the fun and games are really work. Kae suggests that such canine word combinations as "Who the hell do you think you are?" and "I didn't ask to be whelped!" are running through his brain, but she is not a researcher.

Fortunately, the pup's black mood doesn't last long. By his fifth month, his new permanent teeth are all in place, his jaws feel comfortable and his brain is again ready for constructive thoughts. Now the polishing period begins. He's corrected whenever he responds to a command in sloppy fashion. On a sit, his forelegs must be planted straight, his head must be up and alert, his topline slanted straight to the butt, and his hindlegs folded tight against his body. And it is a time for brevity of words and patience. The command is "Bruno, Sit!" rather than the impatient "Bruno, Sit, Sit, Sit, Sit, Sit—Damn You, Sit, Sit!" If the student becomes accustomed to a repeated command, he's almost sure to hesitate when the chips are down and he's in the ring, as if waiting for his handler to set a new world's word record. He who hesitates too long blows his chances to qualify for a leg.

So it goes with all six of the basic commands. The pup or adult dog who knows them and responds promptly is well on his way to success at the Obedience trials. He's as ready as he ever will be for the specific exercises required in Novice. Learning the exercises (Chapter X) is pretty much a matter of routine, of training the dog to do the same thing over and over again. The only danger is boredom for the dog, and Kae averts this danger by adding variety to the routine. At an actual trial, for example, the dog performs his heeling exercises on level open ground. The only obstacle he'd meet would be his own clumsy handler. But in training sessions, he can be kept at heel while circling trees, running up stairs, jumping a wall, or wading through a stream. Then, under trial conditions, heeling becomes a breeze.

Overall, Kae feels that it's the humans, not the dogs, who create the difficult problems, albeit innocently. In her Obedience Utopia, all training sessions would be filmed for instant replay. Then the handler could witness sins that he was unconsciously committing. Perhaps he would be frightened by his own tone of voice, so why shouldn't his dog be hesitant or shy? Or he made a left turn so quickly that the dog had no chance to avoid a collision. Or his fancy hand "Down" signal looked more like he was trying to bat a fly. Or his low bow as he uttered, "Bruno, Come!" gave the dog the impression that the utterer was about to fall on his face. Frequently, then, the eager handler confuses the willing dog. The problem is easily solved by inviting an experienced critic to a training session.

While she may be slightly prejudiced about the Poodle breed, Kae acknowledges that any dog, purebred or mongrel, has the brains to learn simple obedience. The acknowledgment is based on actual experience, for she's taught handlers to train close to eighty breeds, plus a great variety of mixed-breed pooches. Some dogs are as stupid as some humans, of course, but time and patience will accomplish a great deal with even the dullest. If the dog cannot go on to fame in the Obedience trials, at least he's a better citizen and thus more of a joy.

She warns that those who do their training at home must invent ways to provide distractions. If he's headed for the trials, the dog trained in the backyard will perform under par in the ring, where he's exposed to the unexpected at all times. There are easy ways to provide distractions if one has children, or can rent some, or has other dogs. And it's a little more inconvenient, although it pays off in the long run, to enter the dog in a few match trials. There he'll get used to other dogs, strange people, and more noise than occurs at licensed trials. Obviously, the steadier the dog, the more responsive he is to a command, be it voice or hand signal.

"On lead first" is one of Kae's golden rules for training a dog to do anything. Then he's under control at all times and handy for instant correction. Once he has the command or exercise down pat, the student is ready to perform off lead. The rule saves hours

Kae Reiley trains a Standard Poodle student to go over the High Jump (above) on the command "Hup." Note loose lead. After three jumps on lead, dog performed perfectly (below) free of lead.

of time, prevents maximum frustration, and keeps the vocabulary clean.

Overall, Kae has six areas of advice for owners who want an obedient pet or a trial dog. The advice has worked with thousands of beginning pups and advanced adult dogs, and anyone capable of reading and walking can employ them and achieve desired results. The Kae Reiley Six Set:

1.) *In the beginning, keep the dog happy, spirited, and confident.* This is done by keeping oneself happy, spirited, and confident. Don't worry about trying anything to achieve the desired result. In teaching "Come," for example, bend over, clap hands, and repeat the command if necessary. The thing to watch is the word "No." Try to avoid using it, for it usually comes out harsh and dampens the dog's spirit. Rather than "No," help him as much as possible. In advanced work, such as directed jumping, the dog may run for the solid rather than the bar jump. In that case, run to the bar jump, pat it, call the dog, direct him to it. And always, whether he performs in precise or clumsy fashion, heap on the praise.

   Correction at the very start is important. The sooner the dog learns to sit properly, the less the likelihood of his goofing later at the trials. Set a high standard of performance for every command, every exercise. Then, as the dog learns his job, start cutting down on your extra commands, body motions, and tricks designed to encourage him. And by all means, keep up the praise. A dog minus spirit is not a joy.

2.) *No worthwhile learning takes place unless the dog is alert.* This means keeping the dog's attention, whether the training sessions last three minutes or twenty minutes. The dog busy sniffing the ground doesn't have his mind on the work at hand. So when you train, concentrate on it. If the dog needs a break, play with him, keep his mind on you, then return to work. When working him on lead, actions such as an unexpected tug on the lead, a playful slap on the rump, and a nudge with the knee will both correct him and keep his mind on the lesson.

3.) *Watch your timing.* Give the command and wait. If the dog responds, praise him. If he doesn't, correct him (on lead) and then praise. Omit the praise and he'll never know why he was corrected.

There's a great human urge to use a lead correction (tug) as the command is given. While this will teach the dog the meaning of the command, it's also a meaning of unpleasant association, and there goes the spirit. So forget the urge. The correction should follow the command, and only if there is no response.

4.) *The voice is an important ingredient of the success formula.* Use a normal tone of voice in uttering commands, and try to keep it gay. The dog who responds to a drill-sergeant tone of voice does so with the resentful spirit of a new recruit. Remember that a dog's sense of hearing is much more acute than a human's. Vocal volume is unnecessary and costs points at the trials. And there's this big advantage to using a normal tone: it can be sharpened for a vocal correction and keep the dog on his toes.

5.) *If you forget praise, you might as well forget training.* Well, one *can* train a dog through fear, but praise is the humane, easy, quick way to achieve the desired end. The rare dog who won't respond is a moron and probably couldn't be trained through fear. He would probably lack the instinct to avoid fire.

Too much praise may go to a woman's head, but never to a dog's. It gives him confidence, softens any necessary corrections, tells him that he's done something right, and increases his desire to please.

As time goes on, the trainer of an Obedience-trial dog tends to forget all this. He takes it for granted that the dog will always work well, for now he's well trained. But the veterans need praise as much as the beginning pups. It helps to keep them happy and eager. It doesn't cost anything to say, "Good dog," in public. If the trainer is shy, a friendly pat on the dog's head is a fine substitute.

6.) *The thinking trainer has thinking hands.* The Obedience dog going for his UD must respond to hand signals, and not to vocal commands. Right from the start of basic training, the hand signal can be blended with the vocal command. Heeling provides one example: when giving the heel command, jerk on the lead with the left hand, as you step off. The dog becomes aware of both legs and hand motion. Eventually, and off lead, just the forward motion of the left hand will mean heeling to him.

In teaching the stand, wad leash into a ball and hold in right hand. On the command, hold leash directly in front of muzzle while stroking simultaneously under the belly with left hand. Eventually, the stroke, without the voice, will become the natural command signal to stand.

Thus far, we have been dealing with dyed-in-the-wool Poodle people, and there's nothing strange about that. It so happens that the Poodle has always been one of *the* breeds in Obedience, as if originally bred for this particular sport. It was not, of course, but if it had been, then the original intent would have been one of the great success stories of dogdom. More so than most other breeds, the Poodle (along with the German Shepherd) helped lift Obedience from obscurity in this country and then helped popularize it. Maybe the Cocker Spaniel, Doberman Pinscher, Schnauzer, and Shetland Sheepdog—those other breeds that followed the Poodle's lead and became shining stars in Obedience—could have done the same thing, but they didn't.

In the first decade of Obedience in the U. S. A., those breeds and about ten others were the usual ones found at the trials. For some strange reason, owners of a hundred other breeds believed that their favorites were not ideal candidates for the sport. This turned out to be negative or lazy thinking.

Today, of course, we have positive thinking. It is generally conceded that any breed can go places in the sport so long as the dog has average (canine) intelligence and his owner-trainer possesses just a little more. While no one person or group of persons can be named as fully responsible for the breakthrough in the thinking, one of the pioneers was Sam Gardner. A veteran ad-

Sam Gardner

mirer and owner of Bulldogs, Sam startled the Obedience world back in 1955 by guiding one of his favorites to her UD degree. She was Anglo-Saxon Gaiety, also known as Bop, and the first Bulldog to go that far in Obedience.

Of all the recognized breeds, the Bulldog was considered the unlikeliest for success in Utility. Many a hound has failed the scent-discrimination test, and the Bulldog's flat, short nose wasn't designed for that particular exercise. Nor were the breed's jaws designed for retrieving or its legs for jumping. So Bop's success defied the experts, made history, and encouraged the owners of other unlikely breeds to review their thoughts about Obedience. In all truth, Bop did more for other breeds than she did for her own. While the Bulldog isn't a rare breed, it isn't seen in the Obedience ring very often.

Sam's Obedience baptismal dates back to his return home from World War II. In the interval, he has become an oil-company executive and one of the dog game's top personalities. The Obedience set calls him Sam The Man, a term of respect mixed with awe and affection. Baseball fans and their Stan The Man will understand.

The man who proved that Bulldogs have brains as well as beauty is now an Obedience judge. The fact that he is regarded as a strict judge, or a man looking for perfection, hasn't dented his popularity, and he may hold the world's record (among judges)

Anglo-Saxon Gaiety, the first Bulldog to earn the coveted Utility Dog degree, poses with some of her winnings. She qualified with legs of 193, 193, and 197, always against tough competition. Below, she clears the high jump (Retrieve over High Jump, Open) as Anglo-Saxon Merriment, CDX, stands by, dumbbell at the ready.

for air travel to distant shows. He does hold the record for un-planned trips to Havana.

Bulldogs, Poodles, and Springer Spaniels are among the breeds owned, trained, and handled by the Gardners. These days, wife Margaret does all the handling at the trials. Her presence in the ring often surprises newcomers, for writers are not supposed to be able to do what they write about, and Marge is one of the East's top dog editors (*Patent Trader*) and national Obedience editors (*Popular Dogs*).

The Gardners point to each other when anyone asks advice about Obedience training. This is not mere humility, for the truth is that they started in the sport together, developed their theories together, and share both the chores of training and the satisfaction of results. And for our money, they are the only husband-and-wife team in the dog fancy to watch their language around the house.

With due respect for the limits of canine intelligence, the Gardners hold that command words should be used only for the job at hand. The word "Down," for example, is only for that given activity, and always delivered in the same tone of voice. In the ring, and at home, a Gardner dog goes down, or assumes the prone position, when he hears the word. Thus, the word "Off" is substituted as in the phrase "get off the sofa," when a muddy Gardner puppy is discovered on the sofa. In the same situation, we are more apt to swear, employing any combination of words that come to mind. Our pups don't understand the words, but they get the message from tone of voice and jump for safety.

Next to "Down," the "Stay" command is the one most abused in the average household. It means (at a trial) that the dog should stay right where he is and keep all of his parts frozen, although he may, if he must, wag his tail and move his head. But one doesn't mean just that when he orders his dog to stay in the kitchen, or to stay in the car with the windows open as he heads for the bar and a business conference. The dog is expected to stay in the room or the car, but he is free to scratch himself, roll over and move about. So a substitute command is required for the dog when a strict stay isn't intended. Something like "Relax Here" will do.

The Gardners are great believers in the concept that one doesn't give a command to a dog unless one is prepared to enforce it. Anyone not prepared to follow up a command shouldn't give the command in the first place. Thus, when "Off" is sounded and the dog stays put on the sofa, one should immediately employ physical means to remove the offender. Always, always, even at the expense of interrupting the visiting uncle's favorite story, the dog must be made to obey any command. In time, he learns to respond all or most of the time.

Training in the Gardner ménage starts early, or when the pup is about six weeks old. But the training is gentle, and a finished performance isn't required. They feel that if the obedience words are imprinted in the puppy's mind, the words will remain there forever, and so will the proper responses. At this early stage, praise is lavished on the puppy as both encouragement and reward. A typical scenario:

Hugo the puppy is six weeks old, but he doesn't look his age. He wears collar and leash, and is sort of standing-leaning at Sam's left side. "Hugo, Heel!" says Sam, and as he starts off on his left foot, he gives a gentle tug on the leash and adds, "Good dog." Whenever he has to tug, Sam repeats, "Good dog." The lesson is short. When it's over, Sam assures Hugo that he's a very good dog, pets him, and indulges in such remarks as, "If sirloin weren't so expensive, guess what I'd feed you for your fourth meal?"

While conceding that fine texts on the art of dog training are in print, Sam and Marge argue that the surest way to prepare a dog for the Obedience ring is at an Obedience class with other dogs and handlers present and under the guidance of a proved instructor. Over the years, they have attended such classes under fourteen different instructors, and there will be more in their future. "Nothing quite matches the noise and bedlam of a dog show, and the chaos at an early Obedience-training class is a close, if lesser, approximation. Unless he has been preconditioned to confusion, the 200-worker in the backyard becomes something else and less at the trial, with its blaring loudspeakers, barking dogs, and crying babies. One needs the association of other animals and the guidance of a trainer to prepare a pet for the ring situation."

The Gardners on training: "We don't agree that there is just one way to get a lesson across. Dogs differ, and no one training procedure is invariable in obtaining a response. If a technique that has been successful with several of our dogs does not appear to be getting across to a recalcitrant pet, we switch to another technique, and then maybe to a few more, to obtain the desired result. We haven't invented anything new, but we've learned something from each of our instructors, just as we continue to learn things from the responses of our dogs."

On tracking: "We are convinced that any dog can be taught to track. Since tracking is great fun for the dog and worthwhile exercise for the owner, we encourage every dog owner to participate. The earlier a dog is started, the better. We use a litter mate or one of the pup's parents as track layer. One of us takes the track layer, on lead, out in a field and hides. The pup, seeing his associate leave, will be frantic to follow and anxious to find the decoy dog. The one with him obliges by putting him in a tracking harness and urging him to follow. The pup's nose goes to the ground and he's off on his first tracking mission. When he finds the track layer, we provide much whooping, hollering, and praise. We keep it fun for the pup, he gains confidence in his ability to follow a scent, and in a few weeks he's ready to be worked on just human scent. Finally, he's able to retrieve an article lost on the track.

"By the time the pup is nine months old, he should be certifiable to enter tracking competition and then go on to his TD degree. Most of our own dogs have earned the TD before the CD.

"One must be very patient in teaching tracking and never work the dog beyond his capabilities. The handler should work with turn stakes* until well after the dog has established his ability to trail, since the handler must be able to locate the track in the event the dog loses it. The tracking dog must win plenty of en-

---

* An actual stake or anything else posted along a trail so that the handler will know where the trail is.

counters before being asked to take on that strange, blind scent of the test that counts."

While a third of them aren't very active, about a hundred Obedience judges are licensed for all four degrees, and Sam is one of them. For almost two decades, he's been waiting to judge a perfect performance, or a 200, and he's still hoping. The hope may account for some of his popularity, for many judges refuse to admit the possibility of a 200. They may go as high as 199½, but no higher, as if handler or dog breathed at the wrong time and thus lost half a point.

"As a judge, what I like to see is naturalness," says Sam, "the working together of handler and dog as a team." And he quotes from the official regulations: "It is essential that the dog demonstrates willingness and enjoyment of its work, and smoothness and naturalness on the part of the handler are to be preferred to a performance based on military precision and peremptory commands."

He is aware that naturalness is not easy to achieve, especially in the beginning: "The novice handler is nervous and her tension flows down the lead to the dog." Note the pronoun. It reflects things as they are. Women also dominate the Obedience rings. Most find dogs less difficult to train than children and husbands.

"All one can hope is that the newcomer to Obedience competition does not take herself and her dog's performance too seriously, and that she concentrates on the work at hand, without regard to ringsiders. And it always helps any handler, newcomer or veteran, to watch the performances of the handlers preceding her in the ring, and thus become acquainted with the judge's pattern. The judge will repeat this pattern for all the contestants, and mentally preparing for it will make for a speedier and more workmanlike job.

"In the ring, one should be at ease, not effusive but determined to do as good a job as possible. In response to the judge's question, 'Are you ready?,' don't start any exercise before you and your dog are indeed ready. If the dog isn't sitting squarely at heel, command him to heel before acknowledging your readiness to begin."

The judge and his wife are firm believers that every dog, pure-bred or mongrel, should have some Obedience training. It is their gospel, they have been preaching it for a long time, and nobody knows how many scoundrel canines have been turned into worth-while pets because of their enthusiasm. Certainly, every dog in their residential neighborhood obeys his master's commands. And it is suspected that the Gardner gospel has been translated. Obedience is now going great guns in Russia.

As noted, the Gardners achieved the Obedience breakthrough for the Bulldog in 1955. Another breed that hadn't been heard from at that time was the Schipperke. Alert, smart, and descended from herd dogs, the Schipperke was ideal for the sport, but the breed had to wait for the right fanciers to come along and realize it.

One of the right ones turned out to be Judge Corinne Mac-donald, whose roles as wife, mother, horsewoman, and horticul-tural expert filled the thirty-five-year gap between her first and second Schipperke. Her judgeship is in horticulture, not dogs.

Soon after her return to the Schipperke breed, Connie started disproving a couple of popular theories. According to the first theory, house pets do not make good breed-ring prospects. Some-how, the easy living is supposed to rob them of the showmanship and spirit asked of a winner. It is believed that this theory was founded by professional handlers, for the average fancier owns only one or two dogs, and he lacks outdoor runs, and thus the

Corinne Macdonald

dogs are house pets. As for the second theory, it holds that a dog can be only one thing at a time. Either he's a show dog or an Obedience dog. Its chief exponents are breed-ring enthusiasts who aren't quite up to the training challenge offered by Obedience.

Ch. Ebonette Maid, UDT, is but one example of Connie's assault on the theories. Before she picked up all those titles—and no other Schipperke can claim so many—the house pet went to a certain show where she picked up the third leg of the CDX in the morning and the final points for her breed championship in the afternoon.

Not quite as talented, but another record maker for the breed and Ebonmark Kennel is Ch. Toni's Mark of Dark Star, UD, the only Schipperke with those credentials ever to go Best in Show. He, too, is a house pet, and the mighty sire of other breed-ring-Obedience stars owned and trained by Connie.

On the way to his championship, the dog scored one victory under conditions that assured him of enduring fame. It all started at home, on the morning of a big outdoor show, when Mark tangled with a trespassing skunk. Connie, a woman who knew how to meet adversity head-on, drenched the inside of her car and the outside of Mark with her most expensive perfume. It seemed to her that the imported fragrance was more potent than that of *Mephitis mephitis*. She and Mark hopped into the car and headed for the show. By ringtime, it was obvious to all within a hundred yards that the battle of fragrances had been won by the skunk. But now Mark was on the show grounds and a prisoner of A.K.C. regulations. He had to be shown. So Connie took him into the ring, where he went Best of Breed over several champions. She remembers it as "the smelliest decision ever made." On the day, she voted against continuing to Group and took Mark home instead. In dog-show history, he was the first dog to go BOB while looking like his breed and smelling like something else. It's not likely that any other dog, or any dog owner, will want to re-create that history.

"I do not see where easy house living works to a dog's disadvantage" is Connie's response to the theory of canine spirit. "It's

A juvenile delinquent at six months, the famous Mark now gets along with all animals (except skunks) and all people (including breed judges). Owner-handler Corinne Macdonald credits his new, lovable personality to Obedience.

entirely up to the owner—what he does and how he manages the dog in the house."

As to combining Obedience work with showing: "I cannot emphasize enough how the Obedience training helps the dog in the breed ring." The famous Mark is a pretty good example of her thinking. At the age of six months, when she purchased him, the pup was a terror, completely untrained, and a people hater. Obedience-school classes brought him into line. Once under control, he started winning big both at the trials and in the breed ring.

From the viewpoint of animal behaviorists, Mark should have been a lost cause at six months. But the dog's new personality and success were no surprise to Obedience fans. They know something about the canine that research laboratories and computers have missed: patience and understanding will accomplish a hell of a lot. Even miracles.

Training a Schipperke to retrieve an object is the biggest problem with the breed. The same is true, of course, of many other breeds.

Connie gets around this by starting early and taking advantage of a pup's instinct for fun. She tosses a ball or some other handy object, and the pup plays the game of fetch. Of course, she's lavish with the praise. After a while the dumbbell used in Obedience becomes the tossed object. Most pups accept the substitute. For the seldom pup who doesn't respond, a sliver of meat is wrapped around the dumbbell and held on by a rubber band. When the pup retrieves properly, he's rewarded with the meat. This same meat method is used for the scent-discrimination training. The meat is tied to the right article.

In the case of a stubborn dog, and Connie has had her share of them, she has been known to drop all training for a couple of weeks. This has always worked for her, as if both she and the dog returned to training with fresh outlooks. The Schipperke booster is not introspective, however. She's practical about her training methods. When something works, fine. When it doesn't, try something else. When nothing works, take a vacation, then try again. That places her apart from most trainers. They wear them-

The Pembroke Welsh Corgi is another breed Nature didn't build for Obedience work. This is Ch. Devonshire's Royal Flush, UDT, one of three living Corgis with all those credits. Royal Flush also has his Canadian UD. Owner, trainer, handler: Rosamond Hart, one of the land's foremost Obedience enthusiasts.

selves out trying to trick a dog into doing something, never suspecting that the dog doesn't give a damn about their health.

Her slant on the value of Obedience-training classes for the starting dog is a bit different, too. "While this contact with other dogs in the ring is essential, he learns also that his master will always be with him in crowds and at shows, and that all is well."

Although she pleads innocence, the Mistress of Ebonmark represents a sort of minority school in the dog game, and the one Obedience pioneers and the A.K.C. dreamed about over three decades ago. The school believes that a champion purebred should be intelligent and that an intelligent dog should resemble his breed.

But this belief, which would certainly work toward a balanced improvement of all breeds, still seems a long way from popularity. Perhaps the breeders are to blame. Only a few have the Macdonald Plan in mind. Most are breeding, either conscientiously or willy-nilly, for conformation only, and that's why so many champions don't have the brains to come in out of the rain. And then there are those who are breeding brains to brains, and to hell with what the results look like. They are purebreds, aren't they? And damn smart to boot!

Will there ever be a meeting of minds? It's not likely in this country. Dog fanciers interpret the Constitution's guarantee of freedom of religion as freedom for breeding dogs as one pleases.

CHAPTER X

OBEDIENCE: THE RULES

pertinent Rules and Regulations of the American Kennel club § Exercises and scores § companion Dog § companion Dog Excellent § utility § Tracking § what Handlers can and cannot Do § The Role of the Judge § And other items concerning Disqualification, Abuse, Training at the Trial, and Discipline

---

Most, but not all, of the Obedience rules and regulations of the American Kennel Club appear in this chapter. They are repeated in nonedited form, although the sequence has been altered to provide easier understanding for those who may be reading about the sport for the first time. The purpose of Obedience serves as an introduction:

The Purpose

Obedience trials are a sport and all participants should be guided by the principles of good sportsmanship both in and outside of the ring. The purpose of obedience trials is to demonstrate the usefulness of the pure-bred dog as a companion of man, not merely the dog's ability to follow specified routines in the obedience ring. While all contestants in a class are required to perform the same exercises in substantially the same way so that the relative quality of the various performances may be compared and scored, the basic objective of obedience trials is to produce dogs that have been trained and conditioned always to behave in the home, in public places, and in the presence of other dogs, in a manner that will reflect credit on the sport of obedience. The performances of dog and handler in the ring must be accurate and correct and must conform to the requirements of these regulations. However, it is also essential that the dog demonstrate willingness and enjoyment of its work, and smoothness and naturalness on the part of the handler are to be preferred to a performance based on military precision and peremptory commands.

PURE-BRED DOGS ONLY

As used in these regulations the word "dog" refers to either sex but only to dogs that are pure-bred of a breed eligible for registration in The American Kennel Club stud book or for entry in the Miscellaneous Class at American Kennel Club dog shows, as only such dogs may compete in obedience trials, tracking tests, or sanctioned matches. A judge must report to The American Kennel Club after the trial or tracking test any dog shown under him which in his opinion appears not to be pure-bred.

DOGS THAT MAY NOT COMPETE

No dog belonging wholly or in part to a judge or to a Show or Obedience Trial Secretary, Superintendent, or veterinarian, or to any member of such person's immediate family or household, shall be entered in any dog show, obedience trial, or tracking test at which such person officiates or is scheduled to officiate. This applies to both obedience and dog show judges when an obedience trial is held in conjunction with a dog show. However, a tracking test shall be considered a separate event for the purpose of this section.

No dog shall be entered or shown under a judge at an obedience trial or tracking test if the dog has been owned, sold, held under lease, handled in the ring, boarded, or has been regularly trained or instructed, within one year prior to the date of the obedience trial or tracking test, by the judge or by any member of his immediate family or household, and no such dog shall be eligible to compete. "Trained or instructed" applies equally to judges who train professionally or as amateurs, and to judges who train individual dogs or who train or instruct dogs in classes with or through their handlers.

IMMEDIATE FAMILY

As used in this chapter "immediate family" means husband, wife, father, mother, son, daughter, brother, or sister.

DISQUALIFICATION AND INELIGIBILITY

A dog that is blind or deaf or that has been changed in appearance by artificial means (except for such changes as are customarily approved for its breed) may not compete in any obedience trial or tracking test and must be disqualified. Blind means having useful vision in neither eye. Deaf means without useful hearing.

If a judge has evidence of any of these conditions in any dog he is judging at an obedience trial he must, before proceeding with the judging, notify the Superintendent or Show or Trial Secretary and must call an official veterinarian to examine the dog in the ring and give to the judge an advisory opinion in writing on the condition of the dog. Only after he has seen the opinion of the veterinarian in writing shall the judge render his own decision and record it in the judge's book, marking the dog disqualified and stating the reason if he determines that disqualification is required under this section. The judge's decision is final and need not necessarily agree with the veterinarian's opinion. The written opinion of the veterinarian shall in all cases be forwarded to The American Kennel Club by the Superintendent or Show or Trial Secretary.

The judge must disqualify any dog that attempts to attack any person in the ring. He may excuse a dog that attacks another dog or that appears dangerous to other dogs in the ring. He shall mark the dog disqualified or excused and state the reason in his judge's book, and shall give the Superintendent or Show or Trial Secretary a brief report of the dog's actions which will be submitted to the AKC with the report of the show or trial.

When a dog has been disqualified under this section as being blind or deaf or having been changed in appearance by artificial means or for having attempted to attack a person in the ring, all awards made to the dog at the trial shall be cancelled by The American Kennel Club and the dog may not again compete unless and until, following application by the owner to The American Kennel Club, the owner has received official notification from The American Kennel Club that the dog's eligibility has been reinstated.

Spayed bitches, castrated dogs, monorchid or cryptorchid males, and dogs that have faults which would disqualify them under the standards for their breeds, may compete in obedience trials if otherwise eligible under these regulations.

A dog that is lame in the ring at any obedience trial or at a tracking test may not compete and shall not receive any score at the trial. It shall be the judge's responsibility to determine whether a dog is lame. He shall not obtain the opinion of the show veterinarian. If in the judge's opinion a dog in the ring is lame, he shall not score such dog, and shall promptly excuse it from the ring and mark his book "Excused—lame."

DISTURBANCES

Bitches in season are not permitted to compete. The judge of an obedience trial or tracking test must remove from competition any bitch in season, any dog which its handler cannot control, any handler who interferes willfully with another competitor or his dog, and any handler who abuses his dog in the ring, and may excuse from competition any dog which he considers unfit to compete, or any bitch, which appears so attractive to males as to be a disturbing element. In case of doubt an official veterinarian shall be called to give his opinion. If a dog or handler is expelled or excused by a judge, the reason shall be stated in the judge's book or in a separate report.

DOGS MUST COMPETE

Any dog entered and received at a licensed or member obedience trial must compete in all exercises of all classes in which it is entered unless disqualified, expelled, or excused by the judge or by the Bench Show or Obedience Trial Committee, or unless excused by the official veterinarian to protect the health of the dog or of other dogs at the trial. The excuse of the official veterinarian must be in writing and must be approved by the Superintendent or Show or Trial Secretary, and must be submitted to The American Kennel Club with the report of the trial. The judge must report to The American Kennel Club any dog that is not brought back for the group exercises.

TRAINING OF DOGS

There shall be no drilling nor intensive or corrective training of dogs on the grounds or premises at a licensed or member obedience trial. No practice rings or areas shall be permitted at such events. All dogs shall be kept on leash except when in the obedience ring or exercise ring. Spiked or other special training collars shall not be used on the grounds or premises at an obedience trial or match. These requirements shall not be interpreted as preventing a handler from moving normally about the grounds or premises with his dog at heel on leash, nor from giving such signals or such commands in a normal tone, as are necessary and usual in everyday life in heeling a dog or making it stay, but physical or verbal disciplining of dogs shall not be permitted except to a reasonable extent in the case of an attack on a person or another dog. The Superintendent or Show or Trial Secretary, and the members of the Bench Show or Obedience Trial Committee, shall be responsible for compliance with this section, and shall investigate any reports or infractions.

ABUSE OF DOGS

The Bench Show or Obedience Trial Committee shall also investigate any reports of abuse of dogs or severe disciplining of dogs on the grounds or premises of a show, trial, or match. Any person who, at a licensed or member obedience trial, conducts himself in such manner or in any other manner prejudicial to the best interests of the sport, or who fails to comply with the requirements of Section 41 above [Training of Dogs] after receiving a warning, shall be dealt with promptly, during the trial if possible, after the offender has been notified of the specific charges against him, and has been given an opportunity to be heard in his own defense, in accordance with Section 43 [Discipline].

DISCIPLINE

The Bench Show, Obedience Trial or Field Trial Committee of a club or association shall have the right to suspend any person from the privileges of The American Kennel Club for conduct prejudicial to the best interests of pure-bred dogs, dog shows, obedience trials, field trials or The American Kennel Club, alleged to have occurred in connection with or during the process of its show, obedience trial or field trial, after the alleged offender has been given an opportunity to be heard.

Notice in writing must be sent promptly by registered mail by the Bench Show, Obedience Trial or Field Trial Committee to the person suspended and a duplicate notice giving the name and address of the person suspended and full details as to the reasons for the suspension must be forwarded to The American Kennel Club within seven days.

An appeal may be taken from a decision of a Bench Show, Obedience Trial or Field Trial Committee. Notice in writing claiming such appeal together with a deposit of five ($5.00) dollars must be sent to The American Kennel Club within thirty days after the date of suspension. The Board of Directors may itself hear said appeal or may refer it to a committee of the Board, or to a Trial Board to be heard. The deposit shall become the property of The American Kennel Club if the decision is confirmed, or shall be returned to the appellant if the decision is not confirmed.

COMPLIANCE WITH REGULATIONS AND STANDARDS

In accordance with the certification on the entry form, the handler of each dog and the person signing each entry form must be familiar with the Obedience Regulations applicable to the class in which the dog is entered. A handler with a physical handicap may compete, provided he can move himself about the ring as required, without physical assistance or guidance from another person, except for guidance to the proper location in the ring which may be given by the judge or, in the group exercises, by a person who is handling a competing dog in the ring.

HANDICAPPED HANDLERS

Judges may modify the specific requirements of these regulations for handlers to the extent necessary to permit physically handicapped handlers to compete, provided such handlers can move about the ring without physical assistance or guidance from another person, except for guidance from the judge or from the handler of a competing dog in the ring for the group exercises. Dogs handled by such handlers shall be required to perform all parts of all exercises as described in these regulations, and shall be penalized for failure to perform any part of an exercise.

PRAISE AND HANDLING BETWEEN EXERCISES

Praise and patting are allowed between exercises, but points must be deducted from the total score for a dog that is not under reasonable control while being praised. A handler must not carry or offer food in the ring.

Imperfections in heeling between exercises will not be judged. In the Novice classes the dog may be guided gently by the collar between exercises and to get it into proper position for the next exercise. There shall be a substantial penalty for any dog that is picked up or carried at any time in the obedience ring, and for a dog in the Open or Utility classes that is not readily controllable or that is physically controlled at any time, except for permitted patting between exercises. Minor penalties shall be imposed for a dog that does not respond promptly to its handler's commands or signals between exercises in the Open and Utility classes.

USE OF LEASH

All dogs shall be kept on leash except when in the obedience ring or exercise ring. Dogs should be brought into the ring and taken out of the ring on leash. Dogs may be kept on leash in the ring when brought in to receive awards, and when waiting in the ring before and after the group exercises. The leash shall be left on the judge's table between the individual exercises, and during all exercises except the Heel on Leash and group exercises. The leash may be of fabric or leather and in the Novice classes, shall be of sufficient length to provide adequate slack in the Heel on Leash exercise.

COLLARS

Dogs in the obedience ring must wear well-fitting plain buckle or slip collars of leather, fabric, or chain. Fancy collars, spiked collars or other special training collars, or collars that are either too tight or so large that they hang down unreasonably in front of the dogs, are not permitted, nor may there be anything hanging from the collars.

MISBEHAVIOR

Any disciplining by the handler in the ring, any display of fear or nervousness by the dog, or any uncontrolled behavior of the dog such as snapping, barking, relieving itself in the ring, or running away from its handler, whether it occurs during an exercise, between exercises, or before or after judging, must be penalized according to the seriousness of the misbehavior, and the judge may expel or excuse the dog from further competition in the class. If such behavior occurs during an exercise, the penalty must first be applied to the score for that exercise. Should the penalty be greater than the value of the exercise during which it is incurred, the additional points shall be deducted from the total score under Misbehavior. If such behavior occurs before or after the judging or between exercises, the entire penalty shall be deducted from the total score.

COMMANDS AND SIGNALS

Whenever a command or signal is mentioned in these regulations, a single command or signal only may be given by the handler, and any extra commands or signals must be penalized; except that whenever the regulations specify "command and/or signal" the handler may give either one or the other or both signals simultaneously. When a signal is permitted and given, it must be a single gesture with one arm and hand only, and the arm must immediately be returned to a natural position. Delay in following a judge's order to give a command or signal must be penalized, unless the delay is directed by the judge because of some distraction or interference.

The signal for downing a dog may be given either with the arm raised or with a down swing of the arm, but any pause in holding the arm upright followed by a down swing of the arm will be considered an additional signal.

Signaling correction to a dog is forbidden and must be

penalized. Signals must be inaudible and the handler must not touch the dog. Any unusual noise or motion may be considered to be a signal. Movements of the body shall be considered additional signals except that a handler may bend as far as necessary to bring his hand on a level with the dog's eyes in giving a signal to a dog in the heel position, and that in the Directed Retrieve exercise the body and knees may be bent to the extent necessary to give the direction to the dog. Whistling or the use of a whistle is prohibited.

The dog's name may be used once immediately before any verbal command or before a verbal command and signal when these regulations permit command and/or signal. The name shall not be used with any signal not given simultaneously with a verbal command. The dog's name, when given immediately before a verbal command, shall not be considered as an additional command, but a dog that responds to its name without waiting for the verbal command shall be scored as having anticipated the command. The dog should never anticipate the handler's direction, but must wait for the appropriate commands and/or signals. Moving forward at Heel without any command or signal other than the natural movement of the handler's left leg, shall not be considered an anticipation.

Loud commands by handlers to their dogs create a poor impression of obedience and should be avoided. Shouting is not necessary even in a noisy place if the dog is properly trained to respond to a normal tone of voice. Commands which in the judge's opinion are excessively loud will be penalized.

STANDARDIZED JUDGING

Standardized judging is of paramount importance. Judges are not permitted to inject their own variations into the exercises, but must see that each handler and dog executes the various exercises exactly as described in these regulations. A handler who is familiar with these regulations should be able to enter the ring under any judge without having to inquire how the particular judge wishes to have any exercise performed, and without being confronted with some unexpected requirement.

TRAINING AND DISCIPLINING IN THE RING

The judge shall not permit any handler to train his dog nor to practice any exercise in the ring either before or after he is judged, and shall deduct points from the total score of any dog whose handler does this. A handler who disciplines his dog in the ring must be severely penalized. The penalty shall be deducted from the points available for the exercise during which the disciplining may occur, and additional points may be deducted from the total score if necessary. If the disciplining does not occur during an exercise the penalty shall be deducted from the total score. Any abuse of a dog in the ring must be immediately reported by the judge to the Bench Show or Obedience Trial Committee for action. . . .

JUDGE'S DIRECTIONS

The judge's orders and signals should be given to the handlers in a clear and understandable manner, but in such a way that the work of the dog is not disturbed. Before starting each exercise, the judge shall ask "Are you ready?" At the end of each exercise the judge shall say "Exercise finished." Each contestant must be worked and judged separately except for the Long Sit, Long Down, and Group Examination exercises, and in running off a tie.

ADDITIONAL COMMANDS OR SIGNALS AND INTERFERENCE

If a handler gives an additional command or signal not permitted by these regulations, either when no command or signal is permitted, or simultaneously with or following a permitted command or signal, or if he uses the dog's name with a permitted signal but without a permitted command, the dog shall be scored as though it had failed completely to perform that particular part of the exercise. A judge who is aware of any assistance, interference or attempts to control a dog from outside the ring, must act promptly to stop any such double handling or interference, and should penalize the dog or give it less than a qualifying score if in his opinion it received such aid.

STANDARD OF PERFECTION

The judge must carry a mental picture of the theoretically perfect performance in each exercise and score each dog and handler against this visualized standard which shall combine the utmost in willingness, enjoyment and precision on the part of the dog, and naturalness, gentleness, and smoothness in handling. Lack of willingness or enjoyment on the part of the dog must be penalized, as must lack of precision in the dog's performance, and roughness in handling. There shall be no penalty of less than ½ point or multiple of ½ point.

For anyone who has never seen an Obedience trial, some of the above laws may seem a bit confusing. Fortunately, it doesn't take long for one to get the hang of them, and the writing is far easier to understand than federal laws and manuals.

Now for the actual exercises and scoring for Novice, Open and Utility. Novice is for CD, Open is for CDX, and Utility is for UD. For Novice, check Chapter VIII.

Open Exercises and Maximum Scores.
1.) Heel Free .... 40 points
2.) Drop on Recall .... 30 points
3.) Retrieve on Flat .... 25 points
4.) Retrieve over High Jump ...... 35 points
5.) Broad Jump .... 20 points
6.) Long Sit (3 minutes) .... 25 points
7.) Long Down (5 minutes) ...... 25 points
Maximum Total Score .... 200 points

Utility Exercises and Maximum Scores.
1.) Scent Discrimination—Article No. 1 .. 30 points
2.) Scent Discrimination—Article No. 2 .. 30 points
3.) Directed Retrieve .... 30 points
4.) Signal Exercise .... 35 points
5.) Directed Jumping .... 40 points
6.) Group Examination .... 35 points
Maximum Total Score .... 200 points

That's how the exercises are scored. Here are the exercises:

HEEL POSITION

The heel position as used in these regulations, whether the dog is sitting, standing, or moving at heel, means that the dog shall be straight in line with the direction in which the handler is facing, at the handler's left side, and as close as practicable to the handler's left leg without crowding, permitting the handler freedom of motion at all times. The area from the dog's head to shoulder shall be in line with the handler's left hip.

HEEL ON LEASH

The handler shall enter the ring with his dog on a loose leash and shall stand still with the dog sitting in the heel position until the judge asks if the handler is ready and then gives the order "Forward". The handler may give the command or signal to Heel, and shall start walking briskly and in a natural manner with the dog on loose leash. The dog shall walk close to the left side of the handler without crowding, permitting the handler freedom of motion at all times. At each order to "Halt", the handler will stop and his dog shall sit straight and smartly in the Heel position without command or signal and shall not move until the handler again moves forward on order from the judge. It is permissible after each Halt, before moving again, for the handler to give the command or signal to Heel.

The leash may be held in either hand or in both hands, at the handler's option, provided the hands are in a natural position. However, the handler and dog will be penalized if, in the judge's opinion, the leash is used to signal or give assistance to the dog.

Any tightening or jerking of the leash or any act, signal or command which in the opinion of the judge gives the dog assistance shall be penalized. The judge will give the orders "Forward", "Halt", "Right turn", "Left turn", "About turn", "Slow", "Normal", and "Fast", which order signifies that both the handler and dog must run, changing pace and moving forward at noticeably accelerated speed. These orders may be given in any sequence and may be repeated if necessary. In executing the About Turn, the handler will do a Right About Turn in all cases. The judge will say "Exercise finished" after the heeling and then "Are you ready?" before starting the "Figure Eight".

The judge will order the handler to execute the Figure Eight which signifies that the handler may give the command or signal to Heel and, with his dog in the heel position, shall walk around and between the two stewards who shall stand about 8 feet apart, or if there is only one steward, shall walk around and between the judge and the steward. The Figure Eight in the Novice classes shall be done on leash only. The handler may choose to go in either direction. There shall be no About Turn in the Figure Eight, but the handler and dog shall go twice completely around the Figure Eight with at least one Halt during and another Halt at the end of the exercise.

STAND FOR EXAMINATION

The judge will give the order for examination and the handler without further order from the judge will stand or pose his dog off leash, give the command and/or signal to Stay, walk forward about six feet in front of his dog, turn around, and stand facing his dog. The method by which the dog is made to stand or pose is optional with the handler who may take any reasonable time in posing the dog, as in the show ring, before deciding to give the command and/or signal to Stay. The judge will approach the dog from the front and will touch its head, body and hindquarters only, and will then give the order "Back to your dog", whereupon the handler will walk around behind his dog to the heel position. The dog must remain in a standing position until the judge says "Exercise finished". The dog must show no shyness nor resentment at any time during the exercise.

HEEL FREE

This shall be executed in the same manner as Heel on Leash except that the dog is off the leash. Heeling in both Novice and Open classes is done in the same manner except that in the Open classes all work is done off leash, including the Figure Eight.

RECALL AND DROP ON RECALL

To execute the Recall to handler, upon order or signal from the judge "Leave your dog", the dog is given the command and/or signal to stay in the sitting position while the handler walks forward about 35 feet toward the other end of the ring, turns around and faces his dog. Upon order or signal from the judge "Call your dog", the handler calls or signals the dog, which in the Novice class must come straight in at a brisk pace and sit straight, centered immediately in front of the handler's feet and close enough so that the handler could readily touch its head without moving either foot or having to stretch forward. The dog shall not touch the handler nor sit between his feet. Upon order or signal from the judge to "Finish," the dog on command or signal must go smartly to the heel position and sit. The method by which the dog goes to the heel position shall be optional with the handler provided it is done smartly and the dog sits straight at heel.

In the Open class, at a point designated by the judge, the dog must drop completely to a down position immediately on command or signal from the handler, and must remain in the down position until, on order or signal from the judge, the handler calls or signals the dog which must rise and complete the exercise as in the Novice class.

LONG SIT

In the Long Sit in the Novice classes all the competing dogs in the class take the exercise together, except that if there are 12 or more dogs they shall, at the judge's option, be judged in groups of not less than 6 nor more than 15 dogs. Where the same judge does both classes the separate classes may be combined provided there are not more than 15 dogs competing in the two classes combined. The dogs that are in the ring shall be lined up in catalog order along one of the four sides of the ring. Handlers' armbands, weighted with leashes or other articles if necessary, shall be placed behind the dogs. On order from the judge the handlers shall sit their dogs, if they are not already sitting, and on further order from the judge to "Leave your dogs", the handlers shall give the command and/or signal to Stay and immediately leave their dogs, go to the opposite side of the ring, and line up facing their respective dogs. After one minute from the time he has ordered the handlers to leave their dogs, the judge will order the handlers "Back to your dogs" whereupon the handlers must return promptly to their dogs, each walking around in back of his own dog to the heel position. The dogs must not move from the sitting position until after the judge says "Exercise finished".

LONG DOWN

The Long Down in the Novice class is done in the same manner as the Long Sit except that instead of sitting the dogs the handlers, on order from the judge, will down their dogs without touching the dogs on their collars, and except further that the judge will order the handlers back after three minutes. The dogs must stay in the down position until after the judge says "Exercise finished".

OPEN CLASSES, LONG SIT AND LONG DOWN

These exercises in the Open classes are performed in the same manner as in the Novice classes except that after leaving their dogs the handlers must cross to the opposite side of the ring, and then leave the ring in single file as directed by the judge and go to a place designated by the judge, completely out of sight of their dogs, where they must remain until called by the judge after expiration of the time limit of three minutes in the Long Sit and five minutes in the Long Down, from the time the judge gave the order to "Leave your dogs". On order from the judge the handlers shall return to the ring in single file in reverse order, lining up facing their dogs at the opposite side of the ring, and returning to their dogs on order from the judge.

RETRIEVE ON THE FLAT

In retrieving the dumbbell on the flat, the handler stands with his dog sitting in the heel position in a place designated by the judge, and the judge gives the orders "Throw it", whereupon the handler may give the command and/or signal to Stay, which may not be given with the hand that is holding the dumbbell, and throws the dumbbell; "Send your dog", whereupon the handler gives the command or signal to his dog to retrieve; "Take it", whereupon the handler may give a command or signal and takes the dumbbell from the dog; "Finish", whereupon the handler gives the command or signal to heel as in the Recall. The dog shall not move forward to retrieve nor deliver to hand on return until given the command or signal by the handler following order by the judge. The retrieve shall be executed at a fast trot or gallop, without unnecessary mouthing or playing with the dumbbell. The dog shall sit straight, centered immediately in front of its handler's feet and close enough so that the handler can readily take the dumbbell without moving either foot or having to stretch forward. The dog shall not touch the handler nor sit between his feet.

The dumbbell which must be approved by the judge, shall be made of one or more solid pieces of one of the heavy hardwoods, which shall not be hollowed out. It may be unfinished, or coated with a clear finish, or painted white. It shall have no decorations or attachments but may bear an inconspicuous mark for identification. The size of the dumbbell shall be proportionate to the size of the dog. The judge shall require the dumbbell to be thrown again before the dog is sent if, in his opinion, it is thrown too short a distance, or too far to one side, or against the ringside.

RETRIEVE OVER HIGH JUMP

In retrieving the dumbbell over the High Jump, the exercise is executed in the same manner as the Retrieve on the Flat, except that the dog must jump the High Jump both going and coming. The High Jump shall be jumped clear and the jump shall be as nearly as possible to one and one-half times the height of the dog at the withers, as determined by the judge, with a minimum height of 8 inches and a maximum height of 36 inches. This applies to all breeds except those listed below for which the jump shall be once the height of the dog at the withers or three feet, whichever is less: Bloodhounds, Bullmastiffs, Great Danes, Great Pyrenees, Mastiffs, Newfoundlands and St. Bernards

The handler has the option of standing any reasonable distance from the High Jump, but must stay in the same spot throughout the exercise.

The side posts of the High Jump shall be 4 feet high and the jump shall be 5 feet wide and shall be so constructed as to provide adjustment for each 2 inches from 8 inches to 36 inches. It is suggested that the jump have a bottom board 8 inches wide including the space from the bottom of the board to the ground or floor, together with three other 8 inch boards, one 4 inch board, and one 2 inch board. A 6 inch board may also be provided. The jump shall be painted a flat white. The width in inches, and nothing else, shall be painted on each side of each board in black 2 inch figures, the figure on the bottom board representing the distance from the ground or floor to the top of the board.

BROAD JUMP

In the Broad Jump the handler will stand with his dog sitting in the heel position in front of and anywhere within 10 feet of the jump. On order from the judge to "Leave your dog", the handler will give his dog the command and/or signal to stay, and go to a position facing the right side of the jump, with his toes about 2 feet from the jump, and anywhere between the range of the first and last hurdles. On order from the judge the handler shall give the command or signal to jump and the dog shall clear the entire distance of the Broad Jump without touching and, without further command or signal, return to a sitting position immediately in front of the handler as in the Recall. The handler shall change his position by executing a right angle turn while the dog is in mid-air, but shall remain in the same spot. On order from the judge, the handler will give the command or signal to Heel and the dog shall finish as in the Recall.

The Broad Jump shall consist of four hurdles, built to telescope for convenience, made of boards about 8 inches wide, the largest measuring about 5 feet in length and 6 inches high at the highest point, all painted a flat white. When set up they shall be arranged in order of size and shall be evenly spaced so as to cover a distance equal to twice the height of the

High Jump as set for the particular dog, with the low side of each hurdle and the lowest hurdle nearest the dog. The four hurdles shall be used for a jump of 52″ to 72″, three for a jump of 32″ to 48″, and two for a jump of 16″ to 28″. The highest hurdles shall be removed first.

SCENT DISCRIMINATION

In each of these two exercises the dog must select by scent alone and retrieve an article which has been handled by its handler. The articles shall be provided by the handler and these shall consist of two sets, each comprised of five identical articles not more than six inches in length, which may be items of everyday use. One set shall be made entirely of rigid metal, and one of leather of such design that nothing but leather is visible except for the minimum amount of thread or metal necessary to hold the article together. The articles in each set must be legibly numbered each with a different number, and must be approved by the judge.

The handler shall present all 10 articles to the judge and the judge shall designate one article from each of the two sets, and shall make a written note of the numbers of the two articles he selects. These two handler's articles shall be placed on a table or chair in the ring until picked up by the handler who shall hold in his hand only one article at a time. The handler's scent may be imparted to the article only from his hands which must remain in plain sight. The handler has the option as to which article he picks up first. Before the start of the Scent Discrimination exercises the judge or the steward will handle each of the remaining 8 articles as he places them at random in the ring about 6 inches apart. The handler will stand about 15 feet from the articles with the dog sitting in the heel position. The handler and the dog will stand facing away from the articles that are on the ground or floor from the time the judge takes the handler's articles until he orders "Send your dog". On order from the judge, the handler immediately will place his article on the judge's book or work sheet and the judge, without touching the article with his hands, will place it among the other articles.

On order from the judge to "Send your dog", the handler and dog will execute a Right About Turn to face the articles and the handler will simultaneously give the command or signal to retrieve. The dog shall not again sit after turning, but shall go directly to the articles. The handler may give his scent to the dog by gently touching the dog's nose with the palm of one open hand, but this may only be done while the dog is sitting at heel and the hand must be returned to the handler's side before handler and dog turn to face the articles. The dog shall go at a brisk place to the articles. It may take any reasonable time to select the right article, but only provided it works continuously and does not pick up any article other than the one with its handler's scent. After picking up the right article the dog shall return at a brisk pace and complete the exercise as in the Retrieve on the Flat.

The same procedure is followed in each of the two Scent Discrimination exercises. Should a dog retrieve a wrong article in the first exercise, it shall be placed on the table or chair, and the handler's article must also be taken up from the remaining articles. The second exercise shall then be completed with one less article in the ring.

DIRECTED RETRIEVE

In this exercise the handler will provide three regular full-size, predominately white, work gloves, which must be open and must be approved by the judge. The handler will stand with his dog sitting in the heel position, midway between and in line with the two jumps. The judge or steward will drop the three gloves across the end of the ring in view of the handler and dog, one glove in each corner and one in the center, about 3 feet from the end of the ring and, for the corner gloves, about 3 feet from the side of the ring, where all three gloves will be clearly visible to the dog and handler. There shall be no table or chair at this end of the ring.

The judge will give the order "Left" or "Right" or "Center". If the judge orders "Left" or "Right", the handler must give the command to Heel and shall pivot in place with his dog in the direction ordered, to face the designated glove. The handler shall not touch the dog to get it in position. The handler will then give his dog the direction to the designated glove with a single motion of his left hand and arm along the right side of the dog, and will give the command to retrieve either simultaneously with or immediately following the giving of the direction. The dog shall then go directly to the glove at a brisk pace and retrieve it without unnecessary mouthing or playing with it, completing the exercise as in Retrieve on the Flat.

The handler may bend his knees and body in giving the direction to the dog, after which the handler will stand erect with his arms in a natural position. The exercise shall consist of a single retrieve, but the judge shall designate different glove positions for successive dogs.

SIGNAL EXERCISE

In the Signal Exercise the heeling is done in the same manner as in the Heel Free exercise except that throughout the entire exercise the handler uses signals only and must not speak to his dog at any time. On order from the judge "Forward", the handler may signal his dog to walk at heel and then, on specific order from the judge in each case, the handler and the dog execute a "Left turn", "Right turn", "About turn", "Halt", "Slow", "Normal", "Fast". These orders may be given in any sequence and may be repeated if necessary. Then on order from the judge, and while the dog is walking at heel, the handler signals his dog to Stand in the heel position near the end of the ring, and on further order from the judge "Leave your dog", the handler signals his dog to Stay, goes to the far end of the ring, and turns to face his dog. Then on separate and specific signals from the judge in each case, the handler will give the signals to Drop, to Sit, to Come, and to Finish as in the Recall. During the heeling part of this exercise the handler may not give any signal except where a command or signal is permitted in the Heeling exercise.

DIRECTED JUMPING

In the Directed Jumping exercise the jumps shall be placed midway in the ring at right angles to the sides of the ring and 18 to 20 feet apart, the Bar Jump on one side, the High Jump on the other. The handler from a position on the center line of the ring and about 20 feet from the line of the jumps, stands with his dog sitting in the heel position. On order from the judge "Send your dog", he commands and/or signals his dog to go forward at a brisk pace toward the other end of the ring to an equal distance beyond the jumps and in the approximate center where the handler gives the command to Sit, whereupon the dog must stop and sit with its attention on the handler, but need not sit squarely. The judge will then designate which jump is to be taken first by the dog, whereupon the handler commands and/or signals his dog to return to him over the designated jump, the dog sitting in front of the handler and finishing as in the Recall. While the dog is in mid-air the handler may turn so as to be facing the dog as it returns. The judge will say "Exercise finished" after the dog has returned to the heel position. When the dog is again sitting in the heel position for the second part of the exercise, the judge will ask "Are you ready?" before giving the order "Send your dog" for the second jump. The same procedure is to be followed for the dog taking the opposite jump. It is optional with the judge which jump is taken first but both jumps must be taken to complete the exercise and the judge must not designate the jump until the dog is at the far end of the ring.

The height of the jumps shall be the same as required in the Open classes. The High Jump shall be the same as that used in the Open classes, and the Bar Jump shall consist of a bar between 2 and $2\frac{1}{2}$ inches square with the four edges rounded sufficiently to remove any sharpness. The bar shall be painted a flat black and white in alternate sections of about 3 inches each. The bar shall be supported by two unconnected 4 foot upright posts about 5 feet apart. The bar shall be adjustable for each 2 inches of height from 8 inches to 36 inches, and the jump shall be so constructed and positioned that the bar can be knocked off without disturbing the uprights. The dog shall clear the jumps without touching them.

GROUP EXAMINATION

All the competing dogs take this exercise together, except that if there are 12 or more dogs, they shall be judged in groups of not less than 6 nor more than 15 dogs, at the judge's option. The handlers and dogs that are in the ring shall line up in catalog order, side by side down the center of the ring with the dogs in the heel position. Each handler shall place his armband, weighted with leash or other article, if necessary, behind his dog. On order from the judge to "Stand your dogs", all handlers will stand or pose their dogs, and on order from the judge "Leave your dogs", all the handlers will give the command and/or signal to Stay, walk forward to the side of the ring, then about turn and face their dogs. The judge will approach each dog in turn from the front and examine it, going over the dog with his hand as in dog show judging. When all dogs have been examined, and after the handlers have been away from their dogs for at least three minutes, the judge will promptly order the handlers "Back to your dogs", and the handlers will walk around behind their dogs to the heel position, after which the judge will say "Exercise finished". Each dog must remain standing at its position in the line from the time its handler leaves it until the end of the exercise, and must show no shyness nor resentment.

Those are the exercises related to CD, CDX, and UD. So what about the Tracking Test for TD?

"For obvious reasons these tests cannot be held at a dog show," says the A.K.C. So, they are always held apart.

TRACKING

The tracking test must be performed with the dog on leash, the length of the track to be not less than 440 yards nor more than 550 yards, the scent to be not less than one half hour nor more than two hours old and that of a stranger who will leave an inconspicuous glove or wallet, dark in color, at the end of the track where it must be found by the dog and picked up by the dog or handler. The article must be approved in advance by the judges. The tracklayer will follow the track which has been staked out with flags a day or more earlier, collecting all the flags on the way with the exception of one flag at the start of the track and one flag about 30 yards from the start of the track to indicate the direction of the track; then deposit the article at the end of the track and leave the course, proceeding straight ahead at least 50 feet. The tracklayer must wear his own shoes which, if not having leather soles, must have uppers of fabric or leather. The dog shall wear a harness to which is attached a leash between 20 and 40 feet in length. The handler shall follow the dog at a distance of not less than 20 feet, and the dog shall not be guided by the handler. The dog may be restrained by the handler, but any leading or guiding of the dog constitutes grounds for calling the handler off and marking the dog "Failed". A dog may, at the handler's option, be given one, and only one, second chance to take the scent between the two flags, provided it has not passed the second flag.

The Club or Tracking Test Secretary, after a licensed or member tracking test, shall forward the two copies of the judges' marked charts, the entry forms with certification attached, and a marked and certified copy of the catalog pages or sheets listing the dogs entered in the tracking test, to The American Kennel Club so as to reach its office within seven days after the close of the test.

CHAPTER XI

BREEDS, BOOKS, AND BLEATS

The recognized breeds § *Descriptions of the miscellaneous breeds* § *popular breeds, today and tomorrow* § *Dog game odds in breed and obedience* § *Basic books for Dog lovers* § *The multibillion dollar Dog business* § *show superintendents* § *Free Literature* § *A Gathering of sundry items*

THE AMERICAN Kennel Club recognizes 116 pure breeds of dogs. The most recent addition (1969) is the Shih Tzu, the most commonly mispronounced name in the dog game. Sheet-zoo, sort of slurred, is proper.

The breeds are listed by Group:

GROUP I: SPORTING DOGS

Pointer
Pointer, German Shorthaired
Pointer, German Wirehaired
Retriever, Chesapeake Bay
Retriever, Curly-Coated
Retriever, Flat-Coated
Retriever, Golden
Retriever, Labrador
Setter, English

Setter, Gordon
Setter, Irish
Spaniel, American Water
Spaniel, Brittany
Spaniel, Clumber
Spaniel, Cocker
Spaniel, English Cocker
Spaniel, English Springer
Spaniel, Field

Spaniel, Irish Water
Spaniel, Sussex
Spaniel, Welsh Springer

Vizsla
Weimaraner
Wirehaired Pointing Griffon

GROUP II: HOUNDS

Afghan Hound
Basenji
Basset Hound
Beagle
Black and Tan Coonhound
Bloodhound
Borzoi
Dachshund
Foxhound, American
Foxhound, English
Greyhound

Harrier
Irish Wolfhound
Norwegian Elkhound
Otter Hound
Rhodesian Ridgeback
Saluki
Scottish Deerhound
Whippet

GROUP III: WORKING DOGS

Alaskan Malamute
Belgian Malinois
Belgian Sheepdog
Belgian Tervuren
Bernese Mountain Dog
Bouvier des Flandres
Boxer
Briard
Bullmastiff
Collie
Doberman Pinscher
German Shepherd Dog
Giant Schnauzer
Great Dane
Great Pyrenees

Komondor
Kuvasz
Mastiff
Newfoundland
Old English Sheepdog
Puli
Rottweiler
St. Bernard
Samoyed
Shetland Sheepdog
Siberian Husky
Standard Schnauzer
Welsh Corgi, Cardigan
Welsh Corgi, Pembroke

GROUP IV: TERRIERS

Airedale Terrier
Australian Terrier
Bedlington Terrier
Border Terrier
Bull Terrier
Cairn Terrier
Dandie Dinmont Terrier
Fox Terrier
Irish Terrier
Kerry Blue Terrier

Lakeland Terrier
Manchester Terrier
Miniature Schnauzer
Norwich Terrier
Scottish Terrier
Sealyham Terrier
Skye Terrier
Staffordshire Terrier
Welsh Terrier
West Highland White Terrier

GROUP V: TOYS

Affenpinscher
Brussels Griffon
Chihuahua
English Toy Spaniel
Italian Greyhound
Japanese Spaniel
Maltese
Manchester Terrier (Toy)
Miniature Pinscher

Papillon
Pekingese
Pomeranian
Poodle (Toy)
Pug
Shih Tzu
Silky Terrier
Yorkshire Terrier

GROUP VI: NON-SPORTING DOGS

Boston Terrier
Bulldog
Chow Chow
Dalmatian
French Bulldog

Keeshond
Lhasa Apso
Poodle
Schipperke

Literature pertaining to any of the 116 recognized breeds is as near as your book store, pet store, or library. This is not true of the ten Miscellaneous breeds listed by the A.K.C. Any decade now, one or two of these breeds may receive official recognition. To achieve that status, each breed must attract more breeders and more owners and thus prove that it is not a mild passing fancy but here to stay.

The problem of the current breeders, then, is to popularize their breeds: to expose the breeds to the public and to convince the public that the breeds are worthwhile.

The breeders are among the most enthusiastic people in the dog game. Each is sure that his favorite is tops in the canine world. At least half of them dream of making a million when their breed catches on. We wish them well.

But from where we sit, too many of them are missing the boat. They feel that dog shows are best for public exposure, and they concentrate on the breed ring, where the wins are meaningless and the few spectators are curious but not buying. And at most shows, the Miscellaneous breed ring is within a few hundred feet of the Obedience rings, where throngs are attracted by the continuous action. But few of the breeds are ever seen in Obedience. If the breeds are as intelligent as claimed, the trials will prove the point, give them much more exposure, and help to popularize them.

Meanwhile, the average dog lover seldom sees these breeds and wouldn't recognize one when he saw one. Here's what the ten look like:

AKITA

The breed is from Japan, not England, and that's a unique distinction. It's a big breed, with dogs standing up to $27\frac{1}{2}$ inches at the shoulders and weighing up to 110 pounds. A little longer than it is tall, it has a massive head at one end and a large high-set tail at the other. The head features a square muzzle, powerful jaws, triangular eye sets, and short, erect ears that tilt forward. The big tail hooks over the back, sometimes in a double curl. Wears a double coat, the outer one harsh to the touch. Coat colors run all the way from cream to solid black and include various shadings of brown, red, gray, or silver. Limited areas of white are permitted on chest, forelegs, hind paws, tip of tail, and collar.

This is a powerful breed, and in Japan both the police and

army use it for sentry and attack duties. If it ever makes the grade here, it will be in the Working Group.

In this country, the Akita has attracted a host of new breeders, and they've been pushing it for over ten years. Enthusiasm is not always a worthy substitute for experience, however. One breeder, faced with the problem of hip dysplasia in his line, told us how he planned to eradicate the malady: "Through inbreeding, I'll breed this bitch to her sire. Both have bad hips, but the pups will be clean." According to him, two negatives make many positives.

AUSTRALIAN CATTLE DOG

On the range, he's known as a heeler, for he instinctively herds livestock by nipping at the heels. Dogs stand 18 inches and weigh close to 33 pounds. The head is V-shaped, with skull broad and slightly domed, and muzzle medium long and tapering. Tail is carried down when at rest, up and straight out when in action. Ears pricked and eyes oval. Double coat, with outer coat short and harsh. Color is usually a mottled blue with tan markings.

Most of the breeders are found in the West, as are most cattle and sheep. But this is an alert, active dog, makes a fine pet for children, and his reputation as a mild guard dog is increasing. Mailmen are aware of this, but they are not worried. They just wear high shoes to protect their heels and ankles.

AUSTRALIAN KELPIE

Another herding dog, and Down Under he's used more on sheep than cattle. Spirited, easy to train, and with a remarkable ability to learn hand signals, the Kelpie is a sure bet for Obedience stardom, if his admirers really intend to popularize the breed.

The Kelpie is a little taller and a little lighter than the Cattle Dog, so the build appears slimmer. The eyes are almond shaped, the coat color a solid black, red, fawn, liver, or smoke blue. Black and tan and red and tan are also permitted. The coat is never mottled. Otherwise, the Kelpie and the Cattle Dog, cousins in their genes anyway, look quite similar.

BORDER COLLIE

The oldest of the sheep-herding breeds, the Border still carries the head of the old-fashioned Collie: slightly blunt and short in muzzle, with a moderate stop and broad skull. Dogs stand 18 inches and weigh up to 45 pounds. Coat color is usually black, and coat fashion is usually wavy.

Overall, the breed looks solid in comparison to the Kelpie. And it has a couple of unusual features: standing, the breed leans back a little, as if bracing itself; traveling at top speed, the hind-legs are carried wide and straddle the forelegs.

CAVALIER KING CHARLES SPANIEL

An excellent breed for anyone who likes to dominate the conversation at dinner parties but finds himself short on subjects. Today's Cavalier is a revival of a sixteenth-century breed type that went out of fashion for a couple of centuries. Then selective breeding brought it back to what it used to be. The Kennel Club of England recognized it in England back in 1944, but it still lacks the A.K.C. blessing here. The fact that the Cavalier is still waiting in line with the other Miscellaneous breeds is considered ironic in some quarters, for it was an American dog fancier, Roswell Eldridge, who first dreamed the almost impossible dream of bringing back the lost breed.

Dogs weigh from 10 to 18 pounds. The top skull is flat, eyes and ears are set wide, and the tapering muzzle is a short 1½ inches from tip to stop. The long ears are set high. The body is square, or short coupled, and the coat is long and silky, and often wavy. The popular coat colors are black with tan markings and solid red.

The Cavalier is small for a Spaniel, but he is not considered a Toy breed. The old hunting instinct is apparently there, for a breeder we know claims he uses a couple of his on rabbit. We believe him, for he once made the same claim for his Chihuahuas, and we drove three hundred miles for a demonstration. The snow was three or four inches deep, so it was rough going for the hunting trio, but they finally found and surrounded a wild rabbit. The rabbit withstood their yappings for about ten minutes, then hopped away into the woods and out of sight, probably looking for a quieter place. The Chihuahuas started to chase the big beast, but their master whistled them in. It was a sort of moral victory for the dogs.

IBIZAN HOUND

The breed didn't reach this country until 1956, but it has been known for centuries in other countries. Indeed, if the Egyptians are to be believed, this was a sacred dog of theirs as far back as 3100 B.C.

The Ibizan is a coursing breed, with dogs running up to 21½ inches and 50 pounds. The head is long and narrow, with a slender muzzle, small eyes, and pricked ears that seem to slant in any direction. A long, arched neck, straight back, deep chest, and a low-set sickle tail. The coat is short and comes in solid colors (white, red, or lion) and combinations (white and red, or white and lion). The color "lion" is a shade of tawny, rather like the color worn by some lions.

The breed runs like the wind and jumps like crazy. Again, a sure bet for Obedience, but we've never seen one at the trials.

MINIATURE BULL TERRIER

A small edition of the Bull Terrier, standing up to 14 inches and never weighing more than 20 pounds.

SOFT-COATED WHEATON TERRIER

This native of Ireland is a compact little dog, with a long, soft, and silky coat. The color of the coat, of course, is wheaten. Dogs stand up to 19 inches and usually weigh in the early forties. The head is moderately long, eyes appear small, and the ears are set high and dropped. Back is short, chest is deep, and tail is docked.

The coat sets him apart from all other Terriers. The first Wheaten we saw at a dog show may have been the first one a famous judge ever saw. We were at ringside and able to overhear the judge's comment to the dog's lady handler: "Worst terrier coat I've ever seen. Too soft, much too soft."

Of all the Miscellaneous breeds, this one stands the best chance of being the next to gain recognition.

SPINONE ITALIANO

This is the Italian Pointer, or the best gun dog in Europe in the opinion of Italian sportsmen. Maybe. He is a slow and efficient worker and not nearly as flashy as the other Pointers.

Nor does he look as flashy. In body, he's much like the other Pointers, but in head he's much houndier, with big, dropped ears, bushy eyebrows, and a big, long head.

The coat is short and hard. Colors are solid white, or white with yellow or light brown patches. Dogs stand up to 26 inches and weigh about 56 pounds. Tail is docked.

So a Pointer who looks like he's related to a hound is probably a Spinone. A breed with fine temperament and one that is great around children.

TIBETAN TERRIER

Another of the ancient breeds that didn't reach this country until 1956, or almost two decades after it won recognition in England. Some fanciers refer to the breed as the Miniature Old English Sheepdog, but Old English breeders are not among them.

The dogs run from 14 to 16 inches and weigh up to 30 pounds. The body is short and compact. Minus head and tail, it would fit into a square box. The head has a flat skull, defined stop, wide-set eyes, and close-hanging ears. Tail curls up over back.

A Tibetan carries a double coat, the top one being profuse, long, straight, and fine. The hair tumbles over the eyes and gives the underjaw a beard. Coat colors are white, cream, black, gray or golden, as solids, particolors, or tricolors. In both looks and bark, the breed resembles no other Terrier. The bark starts low and pitches up, siren manner. In the dark of night, a Tibetan's bark will frighten the boldest robber. Thus, a fine watchdog.

BREED POPULARITY

Early in the new year, the A.K.C. announces total registrations for each of the breeds during the previous year, and the results become the dog game's popularity poll.

The current standings of the twenty most popular breeds:

1.) Poodle	11.) St. Bernard
2.) German Shepherd	12.) Basset Hound
3.) Dachshund	13.) Irish Setter
4.) Beagle	14.) Pomeranian
5.) Miniature Schnauzer	15.) Shetland Sheepdog
6.) Chihuahua	16.) Doberman Pinscher
7.) Pekingese	17.) Boston Terrier
8.) Collie	18.) German Shorthaired Pointer
9.) Labrador Retriever	19.) Fox Terrier
10.) Cocker Spaniel	20.) Brittany Spaniel

The Poodle is the easy king of all the American breeds, and it's not likely that he will be toppled in the next two decades. The breed is two to one over the German Shepherd Dog, and the German, in turn, is two to one over both the Dachshund and Beagle, which run neck and neck. So the German's spot is also secure for a long, long time.

How will the breeds rank in 1980? Lacking a computer, we put the question to an even one hundred breeders, exhibitors, and judges. All have been in the dog game for at least twenty years, none are in our breed, and some we've never met. Eighty-four of the one hundred responded, and then we had a real need for a computer. Aside from the number one and two breeds, no two of the respondents were in complete agreement. This is their composite forecast for 1980:

1.) Poodle	11.) Shetland Sheepdog
2.) German Shepherd	12.) Doberman Pinscher
3.) Dachshund	13.) Cocker Spaniel
4.) Miniature Schnauzer	14.) Basset Hound
5.) Beagle	15.) Labrador Retriever
6.) Pekingese	16.) Pomeranian
7.) Chihuahua	17.) Yorkshire Terrier
8.) Irish Setter	18.) Great Dane
9.) Collie	19.) Pug
10.) St. Bernard	20.) Scottish Terrier

The current standing of many breeds dear to the hearts of American dog lovers often comes as a shock: Dalmatian (31), Airedale (30), English Setter (55), Irish Terrier (69), French Bulldog (97), American Foxhound (107), and Clumber Spaniel, a great favorite in the time of Abraham Lincoln, in the 111 position.

In Groups, the Non-Sporting, which has the fewest breeds, is always out in front numerically, with all thanks to the Poodle. Working, Hounds, Toy, Sporting, and Terrier follow the leader.

Individual registrations now run close to one million a year, and except for a few thousand imports and adult dogs, all are puppies. Since fewer than 25 percent of the purebred pups eligible for registration are ever registered, it's safe to assume that at least four million purebred pups enter the world via the U. S. A. each year.

Technically, even that figure falls short of reality, for purebred matings occur with great frequency and the resultant litters are never recorded. The owner of a purebred Collie bitch, whose papers were not registered and have been lost, decides that the time is ripe for the sex education of his children. The first Collie dog who trots down the street is invited into the backyard, and fifteen minutes later, he's nine weeks away from becoming a father. When weaned, all the puppies are given away. They are purebreds, but nobody will be able to prove it. Not even the children, who knew about sex anyway, but didn't want to spoil daddy's fun.

The annual crop of new pups (purebreds, technical purebreds, and mongrels) runs around ten million. With canine longevity now pegged at fourteen years, the wonder is that the nation is not already overpopulated with more dogs than people. A number of factors, all of them unpleasant, keep the canine population within limits: natural deaths, diseases, highway accidents, research laboratories, poisoning, automotive safety experiments, shooting, and the destruction of unwanted pups.

Still, the canine population is on the increase. Federal guesses put it at over fifty million. Forty million pets, and ten to fifteen million wild or feral animals.

More than enough pet dogs, then, to make the humble canine game a multibillion dollar industry. Far bigger than the paint-and-chemical-coatings industry, for example.

The biggest chunk of the money goes to the dog-food companies, the manufacturers and purveyors of dried and canned diets. Roll all the companies together (national, regional, and local) and their total annual take is close to a billion dollars. It is their proud boast that the nation spends more than twice as much for dog foods than it does for human baby foods. The boast is both true and misleading. (In distressed areas everywhere, canned dog food is purchased for human consumption.)

Closing in fast on the food companies are the pet stores, pet departments in large stores, grooming parlors, and the puppy farms. Except for isolated pet stores that have been in business for years and are owned by dog fanciers who sell only their own pups as a sideline, most of the other retail outlets are unloading risk pups on the market. Dog fanciers are aware of this, but not the general public, and business is booming. So much so that syndicates have appeared, and a man with enough cash can buy a pet-store franchise almost anywhere in the country. The syndicate, of course, supplies him with everything he needs, from bum pups to booties for dogs to wear in the rain.

For the one nearest you, read the big display ads in the Sunday papers and then stay home. The average outlet buys purebred pups for not more than ten dollars a head, then prices them for whatever the market will bear. Almost any breed can be purchased for under a hundred dollars, or less than the sum it costs a responsible breeder to bring a pup to eight weeks, the time when he's ready for his new home. On the other hand, it's easy to find a store where puppy prices start at three or four hundred dollars—or three or four hundred more than the pups are worth.

Those other billions? Well, it's difficult to think of something that isn't manufactured for dogs. From practical items, such as collars and leads, kennel fencing and food pans, to the ridiculous hats, jeweled bracelets, and perfumes. And for the dog who has everything else, of course, a mink or sable coat.

And the dog game spends money as if it grew on trees. There's a point to it all, but it still takes dollars to travel, to stay at hotels and motels, to buy gas and food, and to stay up all night on the long-distance phone calling friends and saying, "Did I wake you up? Well, listen to this! Guess what? Champion Boomerang Billie won Group today! What? No, he didn't win Best in Show. That old bag Myrtle Dimple was judging, and you know how she hates Afghans!"

Would you believe it? Two hundred million a year on dog shampoos, rinses, flea powders and sprays, coat conditioners, nail polishes, and hair dyes, and more moola than that for grooming. And several consumer research agencies are predicting that Americans will be spending at least seven billion annually on dogs in another five years.

Looks like everybody but the breeders will become rich.

BASIC BOOKS

Back in 1875, Arnold Burgess, editor of the *American Sportsman*, put it this way: "It is not possible for all men to obtain extensive libraries, for the cost of such places them beyond the reach of many. Fortunately, however, much may be learned from a few volumes; and if the student will start with these, adding to them as his means will allow, he can at the outset acquire all positively essential knowledge, and increase this from time to time with both pleasure and profit.

True then and true today. While hundreds of dog books are on the market and new ones pour from the presses each year, it does not require a fortune to stock a personal library for the enhancement of one's knowledge, or "pleasure and profit." The first three of these books will save anyone about fifty years of trial and error in the dog game:

1.) *The Complete Dog Book* (New York: Doubleday). Official publication of the American Kennel Club. Histories and standards of all the recognized breeds, plus routine care and training, first aid, and other valuable information.

2.) *The New Knowledge of Dog Behavior* by Clarence Pfaffenberger (New York: Howell). If you don't read this one, you'll never really know or appreciate your dog. Result of exhaustive research.

3.) *The Dog in Action* by McDowell Lyon (New York: Howell). A must for fanciers, breeders, and judges if they hope to understand the anatomy and locomotion of all breeds.

4.) *The Modern Dog Encyclopedia* by Henry P. Davis (Harrisburg, Pa.: Stackpole). The very complete *Canis familiaris* work. Expensive, but if you own No. 1 (above), a secondhand edition will do.

5.) *Showing Your Dog* by Leslie Perrins (London: Foyle). A little gem that provides a look at English shows, where the dog game remains an amateur sport.

Specific books abound for every breed. The more popular the breed, the greater the number of books devoted to it. It's wise to check with old-timers in your breed before putting any money on the line, for many books are pretty much rewrites of predecessors. For the Labrador Retriever, we favor these:

1.) *Training Your Retriever* by James Lamb Free (New York: Coward-McCann). The best American book on the breed, and regarded as the breed Bible by Lab lovers.

2.) *The Popular Labrador Retriever* by Lorna Countess Howe (London: Popular Dogs). Known as the British-breed Bible. Contains fine photographs of great English Labs.

3.) *Labradors* by F. Warner Hill (London: Foyle). A little book, but a fine one. Some of the Labs shown are the ancestors of the best dogs current in this country.

For those interested in Obedience, these two books will cut training time and lessen frustrations:

1.) *Training You to Train Your Dog* by Blanche Saunders (New York: Doubleday). Some of the rules have changed since the late authority wrote this book, but the basics are still sound.

2.) *Expert Obedience Training for Dogs* by Winifred Strickland (New York: Macmillan). A good bet for those who have had some experience in the sport.

If one's friendly bookstore is unable to supply or obtain the above or other titles, these two shops specialize in dog books and provide fast mail-order services:

1.) C & B Bookhouse, 85 Abner Court, Bridgeport, Connecticut 06606, for current titles of all publishers.
2.) The Old Dragon Book Den, Box 186, Barrington, Illinois 60010, for used, old, and rare books.

Numerous monthly magazines and newsletters cater to the dog fancy. Some cover all breeds, some concentrate on a single breed, and others are dedicated to a Group of breeds. For the purists, this is the most valuable of the lot:

Pure-Bred Dogs, official publication of the American Kennel Club (51 Madison Avenue, New York, N.Y. 10010). In addition to informative articles, the magazine offers a listing of future shows and dates, complete results of all licensed shows and trials, breed columns, any new rules, any new changes in standards, and other up-to-date information. Subscription only.

Many fanciers find they can live without the vital statistics of every show, Obedience and field trial in the land, and they manage to lead fairly normal lives without knowing the names of every new judge and kennel and every word of each new rule and regulation. Their preference:

Popular Dogs (2009 Ranstead Street, Philadelphia, Pa. 19103). Also devoted to the purebreds, but more general in scope, with news from around the country, a superior staff of breed columnists, a continuing crusade against cruelty to animals, and special issues devoted to each of the Groups. Subscription, and also available at dog shows and pet stores.

It has taken a long time, but several magazine publishers are now aware that dog lovers outnumber dog fanciers by an easy 100-1. So now we have canine journals designed specifically for the dog lovers, or for those who may not have everything, but at least they own or have an interest in dogs, purebred or otherwise. The biggest, bravest and best of this new breed of magazines:

> *Dogs,* which proclaims that it is "the magazine for everyone who enjoys them" (222 Park Avenue South, New York, N.Y. 10003). Covers the world of dogs, training and care, the latest research, the canine in history, dog psychology, and just about any other canine-oriented subject one can mention. It also calls a spade a spade and exposes the seedier side of the dog game in such areas as research laboratories, puppy wholesalers, pit fighting, prepared foods, and false advertising. Poetry, stories and book reviews enhance the literary tone of *Dogs.* Subscription, but also available at newsstands, supermarkets, dog shows and pet shops.

FREE FOR THE ASKING

The American Kennel Club offers these two valuable booklets:

1.) "Rules Applying to Registration and Dog Shows"
2.) "Obedience Regulations"

Write for a single copy of either. There is a charge for quantity orders. Other booklets are available for those interested in field trials, another branch of the dog game that has not been covered in this book. It is a world of its own, limited to the Sporting and Hound breeds, and too costly in terms of time and money for the average dog fancier. The amateur is by no means excluded, but a personal fortune and a professional staff help.

Also from the A.K.C.—not free but available if you have a free dollar—is the *Directory of Dog Show Judges,* covering both breed ring and Obedience. Since this lists many home addresses, it's a big help for those angry enough to write nasty letters or foolish enough to send Christmas presents.

DOG GAME ODDS

About a half million dogs are shown in the breed ring each year, or ten times as many as appear at the Obedience trials. This does not mean that the average dog fancier prefers beauty to brains. It does mean that it takes ten times as much work for a fancier to prepare his dog for Obedience. Canis Confucious say most dog fanciers lazy bums.

The odds against any dog making his championship are about sixty to one. In Obedience, the odds are more attractive:

Twenty-five to one against in Utility.

Fifteen to one against in Open.

Six to one against in Novice.

Five to one against in Tracking.

The Tracking odds do not mean that this degree is the easiest one for a dog to win. Fewer than five hundred dogs make the attempt each year, and fewer than one hundred make it. To date, there hasn't been too much interest in this aspect of the sport.

Obviously, the odds for success are greater in Obedience. All it takes is a handler of average intelligence and an average dog of any breed. By all rules of logic, this is the sport where newcomers to the dog game should start. Whether the dog is successful in his pursuit of degrees becomes unimportant later when he competes in the breed ring. There, the training will benefit him. But logic is hard to sell in the dog game, and a typical newcomer rushes for the breed ring. He wants a champion in the family.

Breeds are important for the newcomer when it comes to the breed ring. The more popular the breed, the heavier its entry at the dog shows, and this means a greater likelihood of both veteran amateur and professional handlers. The newcomer's dog may be the best in the ring, but nine times out of ten, his inexpert handling won't prove that to the judge. With the exception of the Miniature Poodle, the dude handler probably has his best chances with one of the Non-Sporting breeds. Then, if his dog takes the breed, he also has a better chance of placing in his Group. The Las Vegas line agrees.

SHOW SUPERINTENDENTS

All the details relative to the staging of a licensed dog show are handled by a superintendent licensed by the A.K.C. If unobtainable elsewhere, information about future shows and dates in your area, plus premium lists and entry blanks, can be secured by writing the superintendent(s):

Mrs. Bernice Behrendt
  470 38th Avenue, San Francisco, California 94121
Mrs. Jack Bradshaw
  727 Venice Boulevard, Los Angeles, California 90015
Mrs. Astrid O. Engelke
  200 Trimble Lane, Exton, Pennsylvania 19341
Roy J. Jones
  Box 307, Garrett, Indiana 46738
Mrs. Helen D. Maring
  2650 S.W. Custer Street, Portland, Oregon 97219
Ace H. Mathews
  11423 S.E. Alder Street, Portland, Oregon 97216
Edgar A. Moss
  Box 20205, Greensboro, North Carolina 27420
Jack P. Omofrio
  Box 2042, Grand Rapids, Michigan 49501
Miss Helen Seder
  9999 Broadstreet, Detroit, Michigan 48204
Jack Thomsen
  Box 731, Littleton, Colorado 80120
Marion O. Webb
  Box 546, 500 North Street, Auburn, Indiana 46706
Alan P. Winks
  2009 Ranstead Street, Philadelphia, Pennsylvania 19103

CHAPTER XII

DOG GAME PARLANCE

Adult	Over twelve months.
Almond eye	Eye set in almond-shaped frame.
Apple head	A rounded top skull.
Apron	Frill of long hair below neck and fronting chest.
Balance	All parts in proper proportions as dictated by breed standard.
Barrel	Rounded rib section.
Bay	Voice of a working hound.
Beard	Bushy whiskers under jaw, as in Bouvier.
Belton	Closely intermingled colors of blue and white, or orange and white, as in English Setter.
Bitch	Female dog; not derogatory.
Bite	Position of lower and upper teeth when mouth is closed.
Bite: level	Lowers and uppers meet edge to edge.
Bite: overshot	Upper jaw overlaps.
Bite: scissors	Outer sides of lower incisors touch inner side of upper incisors.
Bite: undershot	Lower jaw projects beyond upper jaw.
Blanket	Blotch of color over back and sides.
Blaze	Splash of white running up face and between eyes.
Blocky	Having a square head.
Blooded	Purebred.
Bloom	Glossiness or sheen of coat.
Blue merle	Mixture of blue, gray, and black; marbled effect.
Bobtail	Tail docked short.

Bone	Substance; a spindle-legged Newfoundland has poor bone.
Bossy	Overdeveloped up front.
Brace	Matched pair of dogs.
Breed	Purebred dogs, uniform in type and conformation.
Brisket	Area below chest and between forelegs.
Brood bitch	Female retained for breeding.
Burr	Inside of ear.
Bush	Bushy, heavy-coated tail.
Butterfly nose	Particolored or spotted nose.
Buttocks	The rump.
Button ear	Folds over in front, with tip close to skull.
Castration	Surgery to remove testicles.
Catalog	Paperback giving numbers and particulars of every dog entered at a given show, plus judges, judging times and rings, point scale, prizes, and other pertinent data; sold at show.
Cat foot	A compact, round foot.
Character	General appearance and personality considered typical of a breed.
Cheeky	Having prominent, thick cheeks.
Chest	Part of body enclosed by ribs.
China eye	Clear blue eye.
Clip	Coat trim required for showing some breeds.
Cobby	Having a short, compact body.
Corky	Zippy.
Coupling	The dog's body between limbs.
Cow-hocked	Having hocks turned in toward each other.
Crank stern	A screw tail.
Crest	Top portion of arched neck.
Cropping	Cutting dog's ears to make them stand erect.
Crossbreed	A cross between two known breeds.
Croup	Portion of back above hind legs.
Cryptorchid	Having both testicles absent from male's scrotum.
Dam	The female parent.
Dewclaw	A useless fifth toe found on the inside of the legs of some breeds.
Dish faced	Having a concave nasal bone.
Distemper	Most common of the infectious diseases.

Distemper teeth	Pitted, discolored teeth.
Docking	Shortening dog's tail by cutting.
Dog	Generic term for both sexes; specifically, the male.
Down faced	Having a muzzle that inclines downward from skull to nose tip.
Drop ear	Ear that falls forward, hangs close to cheeks.
Dropper	A Setter-Pointer crossbreed.
Dudley nose	Flesh-colored nose.
Elbow	Joint at top of foreleg.
Elbows out	Elbows turned out and away from body.
Entry form	Contract between exhibitor and a club for entry of dog in a show.
Expression	Silly? Compare a Bloodhound with a Manchester.
Fall	Long hair overhanging face.
Feather	Hair fringe on back of legs.
Fiddle front	A stance in which the dog is out at elbows, with pasterns close and feet turned out.
Fiddle head	A long, narrow head.
Finish	Gain sufficient points for a dog's championship.
Flabber mouth	A garrulous new fancier; self-appointed expert on breeds and rumors.
Flag	A long tail carried at an up angle.
Flank	Side of body between rib cage and hip.
Flare	A blaze that widens toward the top skull.
Flews	Pendulous upper lips at corners.
Foreface	Muzzle.
Foul color	Color not characteristic of the breed.
Gait	Dog's manner of locomotion.
Gay	Having a tail carried high.
Goose rump	A sloping rump with low-set tail.
Grizzle	Bluish-gray color.
Hackles	Hair on neck and back that dog raises when disturbed.
Harefoot	A long, narrow foot.
Harlequin	Having a patched coat coloration; black on white, as in Great Danes.
Haw	The third (inner) eyelid, more noticeable in some breeds than others; very red in color.
Heat	Female's season or estrus.

Height	Vertical measurement from withers to ground.
Hepto	Hepatitis, a serious liver disease.
Hock	Joint corresponding to man's ankle.
I.D.	Identification card for entry of dog, mailed to exhibitor prior to show.
Inbreeding	Mating closely related dogs, such as sister to brother, mother to son.
Incisors	Upper and lower front teeth.
Kennel	So long as it houses a dog, any enclosure, box or palace.
Kennel blind	Unable to recognize faults in one's own dog(s).
Kink tail	A sharply bent or broken tail.
Kisses	Tan spots on cheeks and over eyes.
Lead	Easier to write than leash.
Leather	Outer skin of ear.
Lepto	Leptospirosis, a serious kidney disease.
Lippy	Having excessively hanging lips.
Litter	Pups of one whelping.
Loaded shoulders	Overdeveloped muscles pushing out the shoulder blades.
Lumber	Fat.
Lumbering	A ponderous gait.
Lurcher	A cross between two hound breeds.
Mane	Long hair on top and sides of neck.
Mantle	A coat that is dark on shoulders, back, and sides.
Merle	Blue-gray splashed with black.
Mongrel	A cross of mixed-breed parents.
Monorchid	Having one testicle absent from male's scrotum.
Music	A chorus of baying hounds.
Muzzle	Portion of head in front of eyes; foreface.
Otter tail	A thick, tapering tail.
Outcross	Mating of two unrelated dogs of the same breed.
Overhang	A pronounced brow.
Pace	Gait in which the foreleg and hindleg on each side move in unison.
Pack	A group of hounds.
Pad	Sole of paw.

Paddling	Gaiting with forefeet wide, as if slapping ground.
Particolor	Patches of two or more colors.
Pastern	Portion of foreleg between carpus (wrist) and toes.
Peak	Pointed top of skull found in many hound breeds.
Pedigree	A three-generation record of any dog's family tree.
Pile	A dense undercoat.
Plucking	Removing dead hairs from dog's coat.
Plume	Feathery tail.
Pom-pom	A round tuft at tip of tail, as worn by a properly clipped poodle.
Premium list	Advance literature pertaining to a given show, covering prizes, judges, events, and entry forms.
Prick ears	Ears that stand erect.
Puppy	Dog under twelve months of age.
Purebred	Dog whose sire and dam are of the same recognized breed.
Put down	Groomed and ready for the ring.
Racy	Slight in build, long in legs.
Ring tail	A curled tail.
Roach back	An arched back.
Rose ear	A small ear that folds backward and reveals the burr.
Rudder	Any dog's tail.
Ruff	Long, thick hair growth around neck.
Saddle	A dark blotch over the back.
Screw tail	A twisted, spiral tail.
Self color	Solid color, or solid color with shadings.
Semiprick ears	Ears that stand erect with just the tips leaning forward.
Sickle tail	Tail that curves upward over back.
Sidewinder	Dog that gaits with body at angle to front, crablike.
Sire	The male parent.
Smooth	A short, close-lying coat.
Snipey	Having a weak and pointed muzzle.
Sound	Same as a sound dog fancier.
Spaying	Surgery to prevent bitch from conceiving.
Standard	Man's blueprint of a breed's ideal dog.

Stern	Tail of Sporting and Hound breeds.
Stifle	The dog's knee.
Stop	Step-up between eyes at junction of muzzle and skull.
Stud book	A.K.C. record of the breeding particulars of dogs of recognized breeds.
Stud dog	Yes, and he gets paid, too.
Team	Four dogs of one breed.
Thigh	Hindquarters from hip to stifle.
Throatiness	Loose skin under throat.
Ticking	Tiny areas of dark hairs on a white coat.
Timber	Bone.
Topknot	Tuft of hair atop head.
Trace	A dark stripe down the back.
Tricolor	Coat-color combination of black, tan, and white.
Trimming	A manner of grooming some breeds; plucking and clipping.
Trousers	Long hair on hindquarters, as in Afghan.
Tucked up	Small-waisted at the loin, as in the Dalmatian.
Tulip ear	Ear that stands erect, with a slight forward curvature.
Typey	True to his breed's standard.
Weaving	Crossing forefeet and hindfeet when moving.
Weedy	Having insufficient bone.
Wheaten	Fawn or pale yellow.
Whelp	Give birth to a litter.
Whelps	Unweaned pups.
Whip tail	Tail that is stiff and held straight out.
Whiskers	Long hairs on sides of muzzle and underjaw.
Withers	High point of the shoulders.
Wrinkles	Loosely folded skin on forehead and foreface, as in the Bloodhound.

INDEX